Healing A Child's Pet Loss Grief

A Guide for Parents

Wendy Van de Poll, MS, CEOL

ISBN: 978-0-9973756-4-0

DISCLAIMER

If your child (or you) is ever feeling like they (you) can no longer function with their (your) life, become suicidal, and any of the normal grief feelings have become extreme, then that is considered unhealthy grief. This is the time to call your hospital, medical practitioner, psychologist, or other health care provider that is trained to help your child (or you). Do not isolate them or yourself if either of you are experiencing unhealthy grief. Get the professional help that your child or you may require.

This book is dedicated to all passionate parents—

Who are loyal to the concept and wisdom—"Honesty grows our children into healthy adults."
Who recognize there is a profound relationship between children and their pets.
And who embrace a respect for pets as teachers, mentors, and sages.

Our children already know this.

Contents

Gaining Tidbits of Wisdom

Children and animals share a profound relationship that researchers around the world have studied for many years. We can't deny the fact this relationship—between children and animals—is strong and infallible. In fact, it is magical.

Have you experienced your child talking to an ant or their hamster? Sharing with their dog those deep secrets, details of their adventures, and celebrating their joy of learning something new? These are the special occasions that your child will remember and cherish as they grow into adulthood. These are the moments that create magic, health, and healing for a child.

All children benefit by sharing their lives with companion animals—something studies verify. Children will greatly benefit by developing and maintaining a heart-felt compassion with a family pet that is as reflexive as breathing. A pet can impart important life lessons to your child through its life, its death, and beyond.

As a parent, are you aware of all the lessons a companion animal can teach your child? Would you like to have your child share their life with a companion animal, but are you not sure where to begin? Is your child facing the loss of their pet, and would you like to support your child during this difficult time?

These are just a few questions that will be answered in *Healing a Child's Pet Loss Grief: A Guide for Parents*. This book has been written for parents, like you, who are looking for an honest and no-nonsense approach to teaching their child about life, death, and beyond, in an easy and concise manner—with the pet as the main source of instruction.

If you are a parent of a child between the ages of eight and twelve, then *Healing a Child's Pet Loss Grief: A Guide for Parents* will act as your close friend, confidant, and mentor to guide you so that you can support your child on how to care for the new family pet and how to manage their grief once the family pet dies.

Even though this book is focused on the ages of eight to twelve, it will also guide parents with all ages of children from infancy to early-teenage years—from the day you begin to think about including a pet in your family to when the family pet reaches the end of life.

Family pets make the best teachers for children, instructing them about responsibility, compassion, and, eventually, grief and loss. With this book's guidance, parents, as well as grandparents, aunts, uncles, school counselors, and really any significant adults in your child's life, can be sure that your child recognizes and acts on those valuable lessons family pets impart. *Healing a Child's Pet Loss Grief: A Guide for Parents* supports parents in doing just that! You will find practical tools, case studies, and "Tidbits of Wisdom" in each chapter to guide you on:

- How to choose the right pet for your family's lifestyle and your child

- How to introduce a new pet into your home and to your child

- How to recognize opportunities when your pet is trying to teach your child valuable lessons and how to support your child in learning those valuable lessons that your pet is imparting

- How different age groups perceive death and how you can explain this to them

- How to tell your children the truth and not create myths surrounding death

- How to help them understand euthanasia

- How to recognize healthy and non-healthy grief and ways to support your child

- How to help your child express and manage their grief once your beloved family pet dies

- How to find extra support for your child

- How to determine the right time to get another pet

I understand the profound emotions and grief surrounding pet loss, and the importance of providing honest answers to a child's questions about death. When I lost my beloved Samoyed Marley, who at the young age of 12 was diagnosed with nasosarcoma, her friends—that were children—quickly came to Marley's rescue when she was diagnosed. Marley became the perfect teacher for them on how to honor a beloved creature for everything that she gave them. It was extremely endearing to help these children with their experience of Marley's end-of-life process.

Along with my personal experiences, plus being a certified end-of-life and pet loss grief coach I have helped countless parents and children around the world to harness the role of pets as compassionate teachers of loss. I have helped parents get in touch with their own feelings of grief, so they are then able to support their child with love, compassion, and honesty.

Parents, like Sarah and Manny, who'd felt like they were alone with helping their daughter, Emily, with the loss of their dog, Gus, found tremendous support from the information, tips, and "Tidbits of Wisdom" in this book. As they explain:

We, as parents, found this book to be the best guide for supporting Emily. It not only immediately calmed our fears, but it helped us explain things to Emily with clarity and direction. It helped us so much to understand things from why pets are important for a child, to the guidelines it gives for supporting Emily with Gus's end of life, to how to explain euthanasia to Emily, and so much more. When Gus died, Emily was devastated, and we wanted to help her the best we could. The "Tidbits of Wisdom" at the end of each chapter helped us when we needed an answer quick! We learned that the word "death" is okay to use, and honesty is best for Emily's development. We are so happy to have read [Wendy's] book. Thank you, Wendy, for writing this book, so parents can be guided with this difficult issue without getting stuck in fear of making a mistake.

I promise you that when you read and follow the recommendations in this book, you will feel like you have a very clear idea on how to choose the right pet for your family and child, what pet loss grief is all about, how to honestly support your family right away when you first get the sad news, and the importance of encouraging your child to honor the life of the family pet after the pet has died.

Please don't be the family that goes through this experience without using it as a valuable teaching experience for your child. Be the family that steers your child to view the family companion animal as a compassionate teacher of love, responsibility, joy, loss, and healing. Teaching children early in their lives to recognize the cycle of life and not fear death helps them as adults. As adults they will be more grounded in their own feelings and will be more compassionate and respectful towards all living creatures.

This book will help you and your family—as well as other important adults in your child's life—create a compassionate, respectful, healthy, and loving journey for your child and the family pet—from the time you consider introducing a pet to your home to when your beloved family pet dies and your child is distraught. A family pet can bring your family closer together by teaching about life, death, and how death is not to be feared.

To help you create a healthy experience surrounding pet loss for your child, at the end of each chapter there will be "Tidbits of Wisdom," so you can get started right away by becoming an active participant when supporting your child through this journey to becoming a well-adjusted adult when it comes to the death experience.

PETS AS TEACHERS: SECTION ONE

Surround your children with animals, for they are the teachers with purity of heart.

—Anonymous

1. The Importance of Pets

If you have ever shared life with a dog, cat, horse, bird, or any other type of animal, you can understand how amazing their presence in your life can be.

You might come home from a long hard day at work, and your dog is waiting at the door for you with a huge smile and tail wagging; or your horse may come running up to the gate, waiting for you to hop on for an evening ride.

For children this relationship can have an even greater effect on their lives. Children feel comfortable sharing their secrets and life adventures with their pets. Their pets will also offer comfort, encourage nurturing, keep children healthy, and build family bonds.

In this chapter, even before we begin discussing the death of a family pet and how to support your child in handling pet loss, I am going to share why pets are incredible teachers about life for children.

Children love animals, and they love their pets. No matter what size pet your child shares life with or which type of pet you choose for them, pets will teach, engage, entertain, and offer a unique bond for you, your child, and your family.

Yet, remember that children can get super excited about the idea of owning a new pet and will make all kinds of promises to convince you that they are ready to have one. Be ready for that and keep in mind, no matter what pet you choose, it will be up to you to help your child have a positive learning experience with the animal. It will also be up to you to be sure the pet is receiving the best care for their entire life.

One thing I remind my clients—a pet is part of your child's daily routine. It isn't about giving them full responsibility for a pet's care. Instead, it is about teaching and nurturing a child in regard to certain responsibilities in order to shape them into a conscientious adult. Your child will look to you for that guidance, and it is your responsibility to be sure the family pet is well taken care of.

Case Study—Emily and Summer

My clients Heather and Keith contacted me when their child, Emily, turned eight. Emily had been "pressuring" Heather and Keith for a pet for three years. Heather and Keith consulted with me because they both had had pets growing up, yet they wanted to be sure they chose the right pet for Emily.

Emily was a shy girl, and she had some difficulty reading. Her school and her parents researched many different techniques and support systems to help Emily. I encouraged Heather to start searching online for a local library that has story hour with a dog present for the children. She found one in the next town over where they included therapy dogs that offered children the chance to read to the dogs one-on-one and in a group.

Heather told me:

> *When Emily walked into the library, her eyes lit up. She became outgoing, giggly, and talkative to the other children. Which never happens! When it was time for the children to sit and listen to the story be read aloud, Emily sat right next to the dog. When she came home, that was all she could talk about. Keith and I knew it was time to get a dog for our family.*

Together, I worked with Heather, Keith, and Emily to help them with choosing a dog that had the behavior and personality that would lend this type of support to Emily. We found a two-year-old rescue dog that was calm, loved to have her belly rubbed, and would cuddle with Emily as she read books to her. Emily named her Summer because that is when she adopted her.

After a few months Emily was excelling with her reading, and, as an added bonus, Emily's friends would come over, and they would all read to Summer. So, Emily also increased her social skills with the help of Summer!

Attributes Pets Provide

As you may already know, kids tend to consider only the fun of having a pet, which is wonderful and exciting for the family. But to balance that out—having a pet as part of your child's world will also give them an incredible opportunity to learn about the cycle of life.

If you are an experienced or even first-time pet-friendly family, you know there is patience, training, time, and effort involved when sharing your home with any type of animal.

Yet, there is so much gained by sharing your home and by experiencing the unconditional love that almost all pets give on some level.

If you are considering bringing a pet into your home, there are many general yet positive reasons to allow your child to have this experience. Here are six attributes pets provide that I share with my clients when they are considering the addition of a pet into their family.

1. Pets teach responsibility.

Feeding and caring for a pet can teach your child about accountability and responsibility. Even though they may not be ready to take on full pet care, this will be a great opportunity for you to guide, encourage, and support them with the tasks needed to care for another living being.

There are many ways to do this rather than just having a chore chart or hounding them about changing the litter box. Depending on the age of your child, the activity of feeding or walking the dog, or cleaning the litter box, cage, tank, or bed will be inspired and guided by you for them to watch by example.

Of course, it will depend on the age of your child (chapter 4), the type of pet you have, and the pet's needs. Yet, when you choose a particular animal with these considerations in mind as well as determining what you are willing to do as far as care is concerned—a pet can provide a vital role in helping your child develop into a conscientious adult.

2. Pets provide comfort.

There are many studies that show how pets help children. Mary Renck Jalongo, PhD, education professor at Indiana University of Pennsylvania and author of *The World of Children and Their Companion Animals*, and, Gail F. Melson, PhD, professor emeritus of developmental studies at Purdue University and the author of *Why the Wild Things Are: Animals in the Lives of Children*, are two researchers that have studied the effects on children that have been raised with dogs in their families. They also studied how dogs benefit the development of children.

Dr. Jalongo and Dr. Melson conducted a study in which they asked five-year-old children with pets what they did when they felt sad, angry, afraid, or when they had a secret. Over forty percent of children responded that they depended on the comfort of their pets.

These researchers also found that when a child between the ages of ten and twelve was asked what advice they would give to a peer that had a hard time making friends or who was unpopular, the answer was to get a pet, and it didn't matter the type of pet. The children explained that a pet would give the child something to talk about and a shared interest with other children.

3. Pets encourage nurturing.

Learning how to take care of others is another quality that pets can teach children. Nurturing goes beyond receiving care and compassion from parents. It's teaching your child to practice being a caretaker for another living being while that being is young and growing up.

Pets provide a multitude of opportunities for children to learn about the caretaking of others. Playing, feeding, grooming, cleaning their cages (tanks, kennels, stalls, coops, etc.), and recognizing moods and needs, are all forms of care that can contribute to a child's development of the ability to care for others.

Dr. Jalongo and Dr. Melson found that in the eight-year-old group when it comes to caring and nurturing for a pet, boys don't feel like it is a "girl" thing. This showed that boys did not feel intimidated by peers about caring for their pets, yet they were learning the important skill of nurturing, which in many circumstances has been stereotyped (incorrectly) as primarily a female responsibility.

4. Pets provide health.

There are many studies available beyond Dr. Jalongo and Dr. Melson's that have shown that having a pet can result in significant health benefits for children (and adults).

A pet can help a child feel less depressed and reduce anxiety. One client of mine told me about a neighbor who had a daughter that was hospitalized for severe depression and suicidal tendencies. When therapy dogs were brought in to visit her, the daughter confided in them and began to feel better. After she recovered from her depression, she volunteered at the local shelter.

Studies have also shown that when children grow up in homes with pets, children

- have less risk of developing common allergies and asthma;

- have more robust immune systems;

- have lower blood pressure when petting their animal;

- go outside more for walks, running, and playing;

- have fewer doctor's visits;

- have less stress, loneliness, and anxiety; and

- display improved impulse control, social skills, and self-esteem.

5. Pets help with learning.

One of the best ways that pets (especially cats and dogs) can help with a child's learning is with evolving readers, as demonstrated in the case study about Emily and Summer. Children often feel more comfortable reading aloud to pets rather than to adults because of the unconditional love that pets display—and the fact that pets won't stop them multiple times to have them re-read certain parts!

Isabelle, my client, was telling me about her son, Travis, and their dog, Rocky. Travis had trouble reading, so Isabelle trained Rocky to touch the pages of the book, with his nose when Travis was about to turn the page. Travis loved when Rocky did this. Rocky made it an interactive experience for Travis, which supported him to continue reading.

Isabelle also found that Travis would ask Rocky questions, pet him, and even reassure Rocky if there was a scary part— which continued the act of learning how to nurture.

Having your child curl up with their dog or cat to read is much more appealing than reading to an adult, peer, or teacher, particularly if they are a struggling reader.

6. Pets encourage family bonds.

When having a pet as part of the family dynamic, one of the biggest benefits is they can help families grow stronger, closer, and have common interests.

A pet can focus family activities. There are so many things a family can do that revolve around the pet. If you have a dog, the whole family can go on walks together with the dog and share in grooming, feeding, playing, and even bathing. Even with cats or fish your family can become closer with activities, such as watching your cat chase a toy or your fish swim in the tank and hide behind things. Plus, as a family— you can clean out the tank!

Pets, whether they are active or less so, can bring families together through the daily needs of the pet, family activities, and adventures. Sharing the love and care of a family pet shapes an additional common bond among siblings as well.

Chapter Wrap-Up

Over the years through coaching parents and their children, I have watched and personally witnessed the magical relationship that pets and children have. In this chapter, you learned how family pets contribute to many vital facets of your child becoming capable and healthy—physically and emotionally.

Pets have healing powers and the ability to comfort through unconditional love, the easing of pain and anxiety, and the power to give children strength and courage. It doesn't matter what type of pet you choose for your child, if they have a strong bond with that pet, the partnership will grow into an amazing teaching-learning experience for everyone involved.

In the next chapter, you will learn how to choose the most appropriate pet for your child, using research and knowledge rather than impulse. This can be a challenging decision between what you find appropriate and what your child wants. The next chapter will help you with these decisions.

Tidbits of Wisdom

1. *Trust that your intuition about including a pet in your child's life is right.*

2. *An animal, no matter the kind, can provide a sense of profound connection between individuals and the animal, among family members, and between a child and others.*

3. *Animals and children are a natural fit. They offer the other companionship, and the animal will provide life lessons to the child. It's a magical relationship.*

2. Choosing the Right Pet for Your Child and Family

In my practice as an end-of-life coach and pet loss grief coach I get asked this question a lot: *how do we choose the right pet for our child and family?*

As you learned in chapter 1, pets can provide many benefits for children. With your guidance a pet will provide nurturing, companionship, and many learning opportunities to help your child grow to be a healthy, responsible, and compassionate adult.

Parents who want their child to have a healthy and successful experience with a pet oftentimes want to pick the perfect dog, cat, bird, or even a fish. Whatever your final choice the most important thing is *not* to pick a pet on impulse or base your choice on what other people are telling you.

Also, you may already have a pet in the family, so introducing a new one may not be necessary at this time. Particularly, if your children already are working well together in caring for the existing pet and that pet is already an integral part of the family. Such a situation is likely already a very valuable learning environment for your children, especially for the younger child who can learn a lot from their older siblings.

If you already have a pet or you are new to parenthood or new to having a pet in your household, this chapter will give you the tools for choosing the right furry or feathered friend—the one that everyone in your family will enjoy as an integral family member.

When choosing a pet for your child, it can be a confusing decision. There is a balance between what your child wants, what you want, what will most benefit them, what pet is safe for them, and what will be appropriate for your living environment.

Even before you consider bringing a pet into your family dynamics, it is important to think about whether or not your child is ready to take care of a pet. I have my clients consider particular issues and questions, which I'll share shortly, when choosing to bring an animal into their family and home.

Before I share the list of consideration tips, something important to determine first is your own commitment level, as well as that of the other adult members of the family, in regard to caring for the pet. So many pets are neglected and given up to humane societies when families grow tired of taking care of a pet that their child promised they would take care of. Please try to prevent this from happening. If you follow the recommendations in this chapter and this book as a whole, you will be able to bring a pet into your family without regret because you are choosing the right pet for your family.

Consideration Tips for Choosing the Right Pet for Your Child and Family

Jennifer and her husband, Ernie, wanted to get a pet for their daughter, Amelia. Here are seven tips that I shared with them to help them with their decision-making. I will include this family's process along with each tip.

1. A Key Question to Begin With

I recommend that you start by asking your child, "What kind of pet do you want?" Your child can answer this question in many ways. They might want a bunny rabbit, but they may want a unicorn as well. Then consider whether it is possible for you and the family to have the kind of pet your child most wants.

For the most part you want to be sure to consider the environment in which you live that the pet will reside in. For example, if you live in a small apartment, a large dog that needs a tremendous amount of exercise wouldn't be the best choice.

Setting limits as to what pets you and your family are prepared to care for will make this learning journey a pleasure rather than a burden.

Amelia told her parents that she wanted a hamster. This choice was perfect as they lived in a very busy city in a tiny apartment. By choosing a hamster they didn't have to deal with exercising it outside, taking the hamster to obedience classes, or barking.

2. Level of Commitment

Think about what level of commitment your child has shown in past projects, like a sport or a hobby.

- Were they excited at first and then got bored?

- Did your child use their new skateboard once and then left it lying around?

- How clean is their room?

- When you remind your child to do something, how much effort do you have to exert to get their compliance?

- What is their motivation and staying power for activities?

You have more pet choices if your child is focused. If your child shows commitment to certain activities, then their interest should be great enough to care for the pet throughout its entire life.

Amelia was a highly-motivated girl. She did the things that were asked of her and followed through with her choices. Amelia could have easily had a cat or an animal with more activity and needs. Yet, since she wanted a hamster, Jennifer and Ernie allowed her to have what she wanted.

3. The 'Ick' Factor

Is your child squeamish at the thought of hamster poop left in the palm of their hand? What about pet vomit on the hallway floor? Do they complain about the smell of certain pet foods, like canned cat food? Do they find the mealworms a lizard eats disgusting? Keep such responses from your child in mind.

If the aspect your child finds icky is something that is a daily occurrence with such an animal, then you probably should steer clear of that particular animal as your family pet. Instead, consider pets that are of cleaner varieties and less hands-on. For example, fish may be a great choice for finicky children.

Amelia was not a finicky child. She loved to play in the dirt at her grandparent's house in the country. She helped them in the barn with animals and was exposed to a lot. A little hamster poop now and then didn't bother Amelia.

4. Activity Level

Ask yourself if your child is active or more laid-back. If you have an inactive child, choosing a dog can be extremely stressful because your child will be expected to walk and play with the dog. On the other hand, giving an active child a fish may not hold their attention or provide them with deep enough learning about life and loss that pets impart.

Since Amelia was more laid-back, having a hamster that she didn't have to walk three times a day was appropriate. She was able to play and care for her hamster in the comfort of her home.

5. Temperament

Even though you might want to match the activity level of a pet with your child's to ensure proper and long-term care and commitment—it's not only activity level that you need to take into account. The child and the animal's respective temperaments matter a lot as well.

If your child is shy and withdrawn, a happy and bouncy Labrador retriever may be the best teacher to help your child be more confident and self-assured. If your child has difficulty getting still, a laid-back and quiet Golden retriever may be more appropriate to help your child calm down. No matter your choice be sure that the temperament of the dog, cat, or other animal is appropriate for your family.

For example, if your family is more inclined towards breeds, such as German Shepherds, Doberman Pinschers, American Pit Bull Terriers, American Staffordshire Terriers, American Bullies, and Staffordshire Bull Terriers, then doing your research to learn the particular breed's traits and tendencies is important. You want to choose a dog that is suited for family life. Even though the media portrays these dogs as aggressive, tough, and cool to own, they can be great family pets if trained well and chosen with a temperament that is conducive for family living.

In Amelia's case, even though she was very laid-back, she was an extremely busy child and involved in many activities. Jennifer and Ernie revealed to me that Amelia was a very caring person towards small creatures. So they felt that honoring Amelia's wish for a hamster would help her further develop her empathy towards others.

6. Responsibility

This is a huge consideration and one to fully discuss with the adult members of your family as well as your child. If Amelia had asked for a pet that she could not be responsible for, it would have become at least a partial responsibility for other family members to care for, or it may have been given up for adoption at a later point.

Ask yourself and your family, "Who is primarily responsible for this pet?" Make sure everyone in the family is aware of the expectations for everyone involved—who will feed the cat, walk the dog, clean out the fish tank, or remember to buy new birdseed is important to determine beforehand.

Be sure that your child understands the rules and obligations that will be expected of them before bringing a pet home. The idea behind choosing a pet with your child is to give them the learning experience of taking care of a pet, one characterized by honesty, compassion, and love, from the beginning of their shared life together until the pet dies.

Responsibilities for care are best carried out when you are honest and clear in your communication with your child about what is expected. Allowing your child to participate with this list of responsibilities gives them another learning experience that can help them throughout their own life.

Hopefully a suitable choice can be made that both gives the family a pet and also your child a friend forever.

7. Financial Concerns

Don't forget that a companion animal entails financial obligations. You will want to revisit your budget, so the pet you and your child choose will be able to be under your care for the lifetime of that animal.

Take into consideration the kind and amount of food your pet will need and their lifespan. Other costs include grooming, accessories, vet visits, medical needs, stable costs, or the investment needed for keeping a pet healthy for those breeds that tend to have physical issues.

All of these costs can add up, and if not planned for, could lead to your having to give an animal up to the humane society. So, be realistic about what you are willing to spend.

Chapter Wrap-Up

You have learned in this chapter how to choose a pet for your child with the tips and considerations I share with my clients. You heard the story of Jennifer, Ernie, and Amelia's journey, and how they picked the perfect companion animal for Amelia.

Keeping that in mind, you can experience for yourself how careful planning, like asking yourself and your family some critical questions, will provide all that you need when choosing the right pet.

In chapter 3 we will begin to talk about how death is a very difficult topic yet very much part of life, and how a companion animal can be one of the greatest teachers for this challenging topic.

Tidbits of Wisdom

1. *Do not act on impulse when choosing a pet. Intuition is important but not the only factor to consider.*

2. *Matching your child's personality with breed personalities/traits/behaviors, types of pets, and care needed will give your child a companion they can relate to.*

3. *Be clear and upfront—before bringing the pet into your home—with your child and whole family about the responsibilities expected in caring for the animal.*

3. Guidelines for Supporting Your Child

In our society death is a very difficult topic, and for the most part we would all like to avoid it. Yet, death is part of life. When teaching your child about pet loss, it is important to know your feelings and attitudes about death first.

If you are unclear about these, your confused or vague explanation of death could, in turn, affect the way your child views the death and loss of something, or someone, important to them in the future. A pet is a wonderful way to teach children about the cycle of life in a supportive, honest, and hopefully non-scary way.

As an adult, you know there is an end to all life. The thing to remember is that even though you understand that all living things die, the death of your child's pet may be the first time your child encounters death. What this means is that your child will likely experience new and perhaps difficult feelings.

Since children are naturally curious and want to know how things work, they will experience various stages of grief and loss that may be extremely difficult for them to comprehend. However, this also offers a tremendous opportunity to teach them about life and death, and help them be more resilient as they age.

Guidelines for Supporting a Child

Your child will look to you to help them through their feelings of grief and mourning, and to help them understand that death is what happens to people, animals, plants, and other living creatures. There are many ways that you can help your child understand the loss of their pet.

These five tips are the guidelines that I use with my clients when they are looking for additional support with children. By using these five tips, you will create a healthy, positive atmosphere and experience for your child.

Tip 1—*Honesty is critical when talking about death to a child.*

If you are unclear about your feelings on death, it will be difficult to be honest with a child. Nonetheless, it is important to tell your child the truth. Avoid half-truths, generalizations, or the use of clichés or myths (chapter 8).

Your child will ask questions about where their pet went (chapter 9), whether their pet will come back, and why the death happened. By answering with clear and informative responses, you will help them to develop a healthy attitude towards death.

It is important to *not* tell them clichés or myths, such as their pet has gone to sleep, run away, or is living on a farm. Depending on the age of your child, you will be crafting your honest response according to their level of development (chapter 4).

Be clear and honest, and talk about death in simple and specific terms. For example, if your child is five years old or younger, you could say, "Buddy died. His body just stopped working. He has stopped eating, moving, seeing, and hearing. We are all going to miss him."

This was exactly what my client Sahara told her son, Zach, when their pet, Gilbert, died. Sahara had to tell Zach this same message about Gilbert's death repeatedly, but it helped Zach grasp the fact that his pet had died. It didn't scare him or foster myths and untruths about life and death.

By eight or nine, children are able to grasp the meaning of death, so it will be appropriate to explain it in more adult terms. Knowing how you feel about death and the grieving process will help you craft meaningful explanations for your child.

For example, Joanne and Mike told their son, Jason, who was 8 years old, the following when he asked how long their cat, Beeker, was going to live:

> Beeker's body hurts, and he is very old. Beeker has trouble eating, so he is not getting the nutrients he needs. His illness is making him very sick. So instead of letting him suffer any longer, it is time to let him die. Remember, how I explained that to you? We will take Beeker to the vet, and the vet will give him medication that will help him do this.

Tip 2—*Carefully allow your emotions of grief to show in front of your child.*

Honesty is important when explaining death to your child. Even still, keep in mind that since the emotions of grief may be new for your child, when they observe your emotions, this experience will affect them.

When your emotions are heightened, it is okay to share them with your child. You loved the family pet, and your emotions are important to express. Depending on the age of your child, the death of their pet is going to bring on feelings that they have not experienced before.

Your feelings of grief, such as crying and being sad, are normal when losing a beloved pet and are important to share. When you show these feelings to your child, it will help them understand that their grief feelings are normal too. Yet, if you become raging with anger or extremely depressed, those emotions may not be healthy for your child to experience at this time. Extreme emotions of grief are better to express without your child observing.

When their son, Jason, was at home from school, Joanne and Mike oftentimes had to go into their bedroom to express their most challenging grief emotions about the death of Beeker. They both knew it was important to only let Jason see healthy grief emotions, so they wouldn't frighten him. However, when they expressed their sorrow in front of Jason, they all felt comfortable with the gentle expression of what they were feeling.

Tip 3—*Help, guide, and support your child through their feelings of grief.*

Once you know and understand what the common feelings of grief are (chapters 6 and 7), share them with your child and allow your child to talk about them with you. Your child will probably have many questions, so be prepared to explain what happens during the end-of-life period.

Joanne and Mike did this with Jason. Joanne took the list of grief emotions in this book and showed it to Jason. They talked about each item on the list, how it made them feel, and their own experiences in regard to it. Joanne answered Jason's questions and let him know that his feelings were important.

Tip 4—*Grief and mourning are different.*

When you create the time for your child to ask questions and express grief, it will provide a space for you and your family to lovingly create another level of closeness and bonding. Grief is an inward expression of suffering from a loss, and mourning is the outward expression (more in chapter 11). It is so important to allow your child, and really everyone closely connected to your valued pet, to outwardly express their inner grief through a pet funeral or pet memorial that they help design.

When your child can express their ideas, thoughts, and suggestions, they will know that you support them fully. It will help them with their feelings of grief, teach them about loss in life, and help them to develop into adaptable, capable, and functional adults.

In chapter 12, we will talk about how to create life celebrations that will help not only you but also your child to have a healthy and valuable experience participating in this part of life with your cherished pet.

Tip 5—*Be an example for how to move through the grieving process.*

Since the death of your family's pet may be the first experience your child will have surrounding death and grief, understanding your own attitude and reactions is critical.

There are many myths that surround death that we will cover in chapter 8. When you explore these myths, they can help you understand and process your feelings. Also, understanding that grief has a life of its own that can surface at unexpected times will help you be prepared for your child's question, fears, and feelings.

Knowing what normal grief is as opposed to abnormal grief will guide you to a clearer perspective so that you can be fully aware and present for your child during this difficult time (chapters 6 and 7).

Since this may be your child's first exposure to death, know that they probably will not know how to respond or why they have the feelings that they do. As such, this experience provides you an opportunity to be a confidant, teacher, supporter, and role model who is there to listen to and give unconditional love to your child, just as the treasured family pet did.

Chapter Wrap-Up

In this chapter you learned why pets are so important and how they can be incredible teachers for introducing death to a child. With the five tips provided, you will be able to support your child in their first encounter with death and be the perfect role model for this life experience.

In the next chapter you will learn about the typical reaction, as generally determined by age, that children have in regard to death. You'll learn how particular age groups typically conceive the concept of death and how they generally learn and conceptualize. Keep in mind, there can be an overlap among the ages as individual children can develop at unique rates.

Tidbits of Wisdom

1. *An honest answer about death will build your child's love and trust.*

2. *Monitoring your feelings of grief is not "lying" to your child. It is appropriate.*

3. *The death of your child's pet will force you to get in touch with your feelings around death, so you can best support your child.*

4. Age Reactions to Grief and Death

Having a pet as part of the family will offer your child many teaching opportunities. Each pet has a unique personality and will impart particular life lessons and quirkiness, all of which can provide a tremendous boost in the health and wellbeing of your child.

If you have children of varying ages in your family, a dog, cat, hamster, or another companion animal can provide particular lessons to each child about death and their feelings of grief.

In this chapter, that's what you will find—the reactions that children in particular age groups tend to have in regard to death. You also will learn how children of particular age groups generally learn and conceptualize. This information will help you to provide your child with the most age-appropriate support. Also, it will help you set clear expectations about how your child may behave in regard to their encounter with death.

Keep in mind as you read that because children develop at various rates, there can be an overlap among the findings about children of specific age groups. This means that your child likely won't perfectly match all aspects for their age group. They may have characteristics of those in age groups before or after as well. You know your child—how they learn and conceptualize—keep that in mind as you read through these guidelines.

Even though this book is ideally about children between the ages of eight to twelve, I find it important to include other ages in this chapter, as well as throughout the book. This will help guide you with the best approach when explaining illness, death, and supporting your child with their grief because of the possible overlap in their development.

Children Under Two Years

Since babies do not have the intellectual and perceptive ability to understand the death of a family pet, they will react to emotions, behaviors, actions, and changes in their environment. Babies and children under two years old are very much in the present moment yet aware of separation and changes in their routine. Keep in mind if you are feeling sad or a sibling is feeling sad—a child under two years old may reflect discomfort in some way.

Also be aware that if your baby had a close relationship with the pet that died, then they may become anxious and may even search their surroundings for that pet. Common reactions include irritability, constant crying, fussiness, change in sleeping or eating habits, weight loss, and decreased activity.

A client once told me when her sister's dog died, her sister's eight-month-old got very cranky around the same time every day. The mother couldn't satisfy her son in any way until she had an ah-ha moment. She realized that her son would get cranky at the time of day when the family dog used to cuddle with him on the couch.

Children Ages Two to Four

During this stage, preschool children typically view the death of their pet as possibly temporary and even reversible. The concept of "forever" and death being permanent is not quite in their realm yet. They do not see death as separate from life or that it could happen to them. Your child may miss their pet as a playmate too.

When a pet dies, children in this age group may experience confusion, frightening dreams, clinging, bed-wetting, thumb-sucking, temper tantrums, withdrawal, and anxiety. You may also experience them saying that their pet will come back and the pet is only temporarily absent.

Since this age group does not have a full understanding of death, you may experience an increase in questions that may seem inappropriate to you. For example, they may ask, "Why isn't my goldfish in their bowl?" or "Is my kitty coming back?" Their grief responses are new to them, so it is important for your child to feel secure and for you to be available for assurance, love, honesty, and support. Not paying attention to the needs of a child in regard to their curiosity or sadness over the loss of a pet can lead to them poorly adjusting to or conceiving of death.

When questions need to be answered, it is critical to answer them clearly and honestly with information that a two-to four-year-old can understand. For example, explain that their pet has died and will not return (do not use terms, such as "put to sleep" or "lost").

Andy, my client, learned the hard way when he told his son, Jake, that Josie went to sleep and never woke up. This scared Jake so much that he changed from being a child who had loved to go to bed to being extremely fearful of falling asleep. It took a lot of work on Andy's part to reassure Jake that he wouldn't die when he went to sleep.

It is also critical at this age to support your child by explaining that they did not cause the death. You should avoid acting like nothing happened or encouraging your child to get over it. The death of a pet gives you the perfect opportunity to validate and allow the grief process to happen in a loving way that supports the child at their own pace.

Depending on the maturity of your child, it is also appropriate to allow your child the opportunity to say goodbye before their pet dies (if circumstances permit). Of course, it is your personal choice to have them present for euthanasia or even to see the deceased pet. That is up to you, and I will address it more in chapter 10.

Children Ages Four to Eight

Children in this age group begin to recognize death as permanent, yet the loss of a pet can still be viewed as reversible. They sometimes will begin to feel as if their behavior caused the death and may even have the concept that negative thoughts or feelings they had towards their pet caused the death.

I have seen in my coaching practice that a child in this age range may experience guilt for being angry at a pet as they were dying. Even though children at this age are exposed to death through school and media, they often believe if they, themselves, were careful, then death could have been avoided.

Even though they may have a better understanding of pet loss and its implications, their coping abilities are still very limited. Denial is very prominent, and acting as if nothing happened is common.

Your child during this age may even hide their own feelings when their pet dies. These behaviors are normal and do not reflect that your child is uncaring or unaffected by the fact their pet died. They may be mirroring your grief reaction, particularly if you are feeling uncertain about how to express your own feelings. We will talk more about grief in chapters 6 and 7—how you can recognize normal emotional, physical, and spiritual signs and stages of grief, both in yourself and in your child.

In order for your child to feel supported after losing their pet, be sure you are nurturing them with their feelings of grief and validating their feelings. Allow them to progress naturally and at their own pace. Try not to ask them to get over it or act as if nothing happened. They will mimic you at this point, so it is critical to set a healthy and emotional reaction about the loss of their pet in order for them to learn.

Helping your child remember their pet when the animal was a happy and healthy family member is okay and healthy to do as long as you still allow your child to feel and experience their sadness.

Children Ages Eight to Twelve

Even though children of this age group know that death can happen to anyone and there are many things that can cause death, it is still difficult for them to believe death can happen to them or their pets. They can have trouble accepting the loss of their pet and will begin to experience "adult" grief and grief stages.

When they reach the ages of ten to twelve, children are active in establishing their own identity and gaining increased independence from their parents. They become more dependent on their friends. This is a great age for them to understand the biological facts of death in addition to their feelings around grief.

Children will also cover up their feelings, so they don't appear different from or vulnerable in front of their friends. This age group can feel that expressing sadness or grief may be a sign of weakness. Be aware they may have questions regarding cultural beliefs and spiritual beliefs surrounding death.

Case Study—Fiona and Cleo

Oscar and Nicole reached out to me when their daughter Fiona's cat, Cleo, died. They called me because they were concerned about how Fiona was responding. They told me that Fiona started to worry that the both of them would die too. Fiona also started to say things that indicated she was worried about her own health.

Fiona started to act out her sadness and concerns by being disruptive in school, whereas prior to Cleo's death Fiona had been a very good student. Fiona became afraid that something might happen on the way to school that would hurt her and make her go to the hospital like Cleo did during her last few days of life. They also found a story that Fiona was writing about a little girl not letting her cat die.

The first thing I assured Oscar and Nicole of: all of these reactions are normal. I then helped Oscar and Nicole determine how they would support Fiona through her grief. This is what they did: they encouraged Fiona and gave her opportunities to mourn (chapter 11) and grieve (chapter 6) to discourage her from withdrawing and becoming anti-social. They encouraged healthy discussions about death while reminiscing about all the wonderful and fun adventures they'd shared with Cleo. In this way, they guided Fiona to experience a full and healthy mourning for Cleo.

Chapter Wrap-Up

In this chapter you learned how children from infancy to teenaged years develop and conceive of death. You also read how pets can support and nurture children during their development. No matter what type of pet your child shares life with, the animal imparts special gifts to children and provides amazing opportunities for teaching compassion, trust, and self-worth.

Through the case study you learned how Oscar and Nicole supported Fiona in developing her own unique understanding of death and to understand that her feelings of loss and grief were normal.

In chapter 5 you will learn that children need a very concrete yet safe way to share their feelings with you. Since life is just beginning for them and so much is yet to be explored, your child is only beginning to learn how to identify and what to do with their feelings. I am going to share with you ways to help your child to express grief and mourn for their pet.

Tidbits of Wisdom

1. *As your child matures, their level of understanding of life, love, and loss can develop into normality—particularly with your support and by your example.*

2. *Be patient with your child as they learn to conceive of death. It is new for them.*

3. *Stay cognizant of your child's maturity level as they adjust to the death of their pet.*

5. Creative Ways to Feel Safe

One thing that I have found when working with children is that they need a concrete yet safe way to share their feelings. Since life is just beginning for them and so much is yet to be explored, your child is only beginning to learn how to identify and what to do with their feelings.

Children experiencing grief may express themselves by acting out, maybe even in a disruptive way, yet there are some simple and fun ways that can help them express and mourn the grief of their pet.

In this chapter you will learn about some fun and effective ways to encourage children to express themselves when faced with sadness or other feelings of grief. Keep in mind that grief is different for everyone. Use this chapter as a guide to help you and your child express feelings and pay tribute to a pet through mourning.

One piece of advice I give clients is to first take a look around your child's space and notice the items that your child already has. Then you can determine whether any of these items could help your child express and creatively celebrate the life they still have or had with their beloved animal companion.

These materials may be:

- Paper
- Crayons
- Markers
- Clay
- Paper bags
- Puppets
- Dolls
- Stuffed animals
- Books
- Diary
- Music
- Recorder
- Musical instrument
- Magazines
- Coloring books
- Posters
- Balloons
- Rocks
- Feathers
- Seashells
- Leaves

After taking notice of these items, you can then support your child in feeling comfortable by guiding them to create a tribute or experience from these materials that honors the family pet. Consider the following that together you could create or do in honor of the family animal:

- Walks in nature
- Books
- Drawings
- Writings
- Collages
- Sculpture

- Plays
- Scrapbooks
- Games
- Stories

The possibilities are endless in what you can guide your child to create or experience to help them to express their grief and cope appropriately. There are many lessons to be learned from these creations and experiences that your child will carry into adulthood and hopefully teach to their children.

Walks in Nature

If your child loves the outdoors and is comfortable, a great way to show your support is to take them for a walk in the park, the woods, or on the beach. This will give you the opportunity to talk together in an engaging environment, which, in turn, can help you get the point across to them that death is a reality.

Nature provides all types of opportunities to talk about death, such as finding dead leaves, insects, or other animals. As you observe these once-living things in nature, you can help your child by relating how these things were once alive and now dead—and the cycle of life and death itself. You can talk with them about the difference between being alive and being dead, always keeping in mind the age and maturity level of your child (chapters 3 and 4).

Books

If your child loves books and loves to have you read to them, finding a book that deals with death in general or the death of a pet can be very helpful, especially if it is age-appropriate for your child. Reading a book to your child offers a great opportunity to explain death if you have a hard time finding words to describe death in a healthy way.

When you read a well-written children's book to your child, it can help them with understanding reality and not making death a fantasy. This is a normal and bonding experience for you and your child as it will open up the dialogue to talk about pet death and even the deaths of other loved ones in general.

I even had children read these books to their dying pet as a means for the children to understand and share their grief with their pet. This experience alone can open up a huge dialogue.

I will share some of my favorite books, and their associated age-levels, in the "Resources" section of this book.

Case Study—Vera and Ricky

Martin and Lana were having a very difficult time explaining the death of Vera's bird to her. Everyone in the family was devastated when Ricky died. Ricky was a parrot that talked, ate with the family, and was very much a part of the family dynamics.

Martin and Lana's feelings of grief were raw and intense. Even though they wanted to be honest with Vera, they felt they couldn't find the words to teach her about Ricky's death.

When I suggested a few books that they could read aloud to Vera, they found it was easier to start an open dialogue together as a family.

Drawings

As you may already have experienced with your child, drawing is a very comfortable way for children to express themselves. It is an excellent tool for many different types of grief emotions.

You can help your child by encouraging them to draw something about their pet that makes them feel sad or angry. As they are drawing, ask your child questions, "What are you drawing?" "Why are you using that color?" "Why is Max running after his ball?"

These questions help open a dialogue that will allow your child to trust you. After they draw a picture that makes them feel sad or angry, you can simply listen while they talk about it. Their next picture could be of their pet and something that made them happy. In this way they learn that the confusing feelings are okay to have and that they are safe and validated in discussing their feelings with you.

Writing

If you have a child that loves to write, I encourage you to help them write a love letter to their pet. This is a very important exercise because your child will be given a chance to express how much they loved their pet as well as any other feelings or questions they may have.

A love letter provides a very special way of healing grief. It is a different way to tell their pet how much they loved them by expressing their memories, experiences, and gratitude for all the things they shared with their companion.

You will read some examples of these love letters in chapter 13, written by a few of my clients' children. They are sweet and compassionate as the children share the tender moments of love, companionship, and trust.

Collages

If your child has magazines scattered around their room and photos of their pet stored on the computer or smart phone, helping them create a collage from these images is a wonderful way for them to express themselves. Especially, if they are artistic.

Like drawing, creating a collage entails an expression of a lot of feelings. You'll find it has a great impact on your child, especially in regard to the building of trust. Plus, it opens the dialogue for them to share what they are feeling with you. This is a great activity for various age groups, and I have seen some beautiful collages that serve as impressive testimonials concerning the increasing richness of a bond shared between a child and their pet.

When your child sees pictures of themselves with their pet, it can be very consoling and healing. Memories are shared, and they begin to voice how important their animal friend was to them.

Sculpture

Playing with clay is a wonderful way for your child to engage with their feelings. Clay oftentimes needs softening, so when the child works with the clay, their energy too gets the opportunity to soften.

Your child could build a sculpture of their pet or a sculpture that portrays their emotions. It gives you the chance to teach your child ways to manipulate the clay and make various objects that illustrate the relationship they had with their pet. This exercise will also help them open up for discussion, especially if you are guiding them and they love to work with clay.

Plays

Children love to act. It is natural for them, and it is a great opportunity to express what they are going through.

You can encourage them to write a play about something special they did with their pet that is ill or has died. The actions and words they include in their play will give you the perfect opportunity for follow-up conversations and support.

With today's multiple technological offerings, you can easily capture the play on video and watch that video as a family, and from there have a rich family discussion.

Puppets

Puppets are a great way for your child to express what they are feeling. If you are the "puppet-master," it gives them the opportunity to say to that puppet you are holding what they feel. They are talking to the puppet rather than you.

Puppet activities make tremendous opportunities for creativity, open dialogue, and safety. It also provides a great space for children to not feel pressured.

Scrapbooks

Putting together a scrapbook about their pet can be a wonderful thing you and your child can do together. It helps to alleviate depression and sadness, especially if your child is really into scrapbooking. And it will preserve the memory of their pet in a format that they will have forever.

In chapter 13 we'll revisit scrapbooking and all that it entails. For now, consider scrapbooking a fabulous exercise for opening and maintaining a flowing and loving dialogue between you and your child. Also a scrapbook can offer many things they may have forgotten about their pet and at the same time highlight favorite memories.

Here are some items you can include in a scrapbook:

- Photos
- Short stories
- Poems
- Adoption papers
- Collars
- A lock of the pet's fur

- Feathers
- Birth certificate
- Packaging labels of their food
- Ribbons, pins, buttons
- Articles from the internet or newspaper about the breed or type of animal
- List of favorite toys and treats

Games

Games are great for younger children. A simple game that I find helpful for my younger clients is to encourage their parents to play the game, "I Remember When . . ."

Here is an example of what Clara's (age 5) parents played with her;

Clara's parents: I remember when you gave the ball to Lucy!

Clara: I remember when Lucy licked my face!

Clara's parents: I remember when Lucy dribbled water on the floor!

Clara: I remember when Lucy ate my sock! . . . I remember when Lucy tickled me! . . . I remember when Lucy ran after the squirrel!

This game helped Clara's parent teach her that Lucy had died (see ways to talk to a five-year-old about death in chapter 4), which allowed Clara the understanding that she didn't need to be afraid that she was going to die even though Lucy had died. The game also allowed Clara to remember fun and positive memories of Lucy.

Chapter Wrap-Up

The idea that all life ends is a concept that your child may have yet to experience. It is probably the most difficult truth we have to share with our children.

Since children flourish with honesty and creativity, there are ways that you can help them talk about what they are feeling. Now is the time to honestly and directly support your child because they are only just starting to learn how to identify and what to do with their feelings in regard to their pet's illness or death.

In guiding them with the creative outlets, keep in mind to support them through their unique process—don't force or push. Just breathe and help them honor the life they had with their pet—and any feelings they may experience as a result of the pet's death. The experiences that they had with their pet are the perfect teacher for them.

In chapter 6 I am going to help you understand what normal grief is and how you can support your child with the feelings that they are going to experience. This chapter will begin the section that addresses helping children through the journey of pet loss so that they can develop into healthy, capable, emotionally mature adults.

Tidbits of Wisdom

1. *The death of your child's pet can be a window for them to express new experiences—support them through this new experience by using what is already familiar to them from their surroundings.*

2. *Guide your child gently with their creations.*

3. *Create along with them—your grief will begin to heal too, and you'll provide a positive example to them of engaging with grief feelings.*

HELPING CHILDREN WITH PET LOSS: SECTION TWO

There's a bit of magic in everything, and some loss to even things out.

—Lou Reed

6. A Child's Experience of Grief

A very common question that I receive from parents is "Do children really grieve?" This is a great question, and the quick answer is—yes! Grief is a normal reaction for children to have when their significant pet dies.

In this chapter, I am going to outline the normal feelings of grief that children experience, which are not very different from those normal grief feelings that you, as an adult, may experience. Even though it is normal for a child to miss their pet that died and experience adult-like feelings of grief, you might not always see or understand the signs. Keep in mind that their grief may come and go with differing levels of intensity for some time after the death.

Adults usually have a clearer idea of the finality of death and will feel grief more intensely and more compactly in comparison to children. Children, since they have not had as many experiences with death or may not be cognitively ready to understand death as we do, will grieve with less comprehension of what is happening with them.

When a child experiences the death of a pet, their grief reactions will be varied, wide-ranging, and unique to the child. Their grief intensity will reflect how deep their relationship was with their pet, and, as mentioned in chapter 3, it is important for children to know the truth about death, so they are not confused by their feelings.

Glossing over the words "dead," "die," or "death" will create myths in your child's world that can result in a huge, negative disconnect between them and their feelings. Even though you may want to protect your child by not using direct words and instead saying, "Patches went to sleep," "Rusty ran away," "Max is living on a farm," or "Zoe is in another place," unfortunately, in doing so, you are not alleviating their sadness about losing their pet. Instead, you will confuse them about what really happened, and they may think the grief feelings they are experiencing are wrong and bad. In fact, if your child learns the truth of what happened to their pet, even years later as an adult, they may be extremely angry and hurt that you lied to them.

These statements can also cause children to be afraid, especially the phrase "going to sleep." This could set up a great fear in a child to go to sleep because, like their dog Patches, they may end up sleeping forever.

Even though it is challenging to share the truth about death, honest answers build trust, help provide understanding, and allow children to feel more comfortable to approach you with questions and more comfortable with the confusing and intense grief feelings they may experience.

Like anyone dealing with pet loss, kids will feel a variety of emotions besides sadness after the death of their pet. They may feel incredibly lonely, or even angry, especially if their pet was euthanized. Or they may feel frustrated that their pet couldn't get better and feel guilty because they couldn't offer their pet help.

You are in the position to help your child understand that it is natural to have these emotions and that these emotions are important to recognize and experience. Encourage them that they don't have to talk about their feelings right away, and when they are ready, you are there to listen. If you have another pet in your household, that pet will oftentimes be the recipient of that conversation.

Also keep in mind that you do not have to hide your own sadness, as we talked about in chapter 3. Sharing with your child how you feel and talking about it with them in an honest way sets a beautiful example. This can be very comforting to your child to help them not feel alone in their sadness. When you share stories about the pets you had and lost and how difficult it was to say goodbye, it will only build trust and compassion—and allow them to recognize and engage with their own feelings, thus building positive emotional health.

Case Study—Peter, Rebecca, and Knox

Isabelle was very concerned when her twelve-year-old twins, Peter and Rebecca, learned that their dog, Knox, was going to die. This news was new and unexpected. Knox had cancer. Yet, Knox still had a lot of life and energy, so the twins reacted in a very normal way—they increased their time and activity with Knox (see below under "Normal Emotional Behaviors"). They acted as if everything was okay, yet they started to show a curiosity about death, as this was the first time they were experiencing it.

Isabelle didn't realize this was normal grief and was worried when we talked. I assured and encouraged her to let Peter and Rebecca spend "extra" time with Knox, as this would give her the opportunity to support them with their feelings and what they were going through.

Normal and Healthy Grief

Below is a brief list of normal and healthy grief behaviors and feelings. I will outline more feelings in chapter 7 when presenting the stages of grief you may see your child experience.

As you can see by the following lists, normal grief is varied and expansive. The thing about grief is that it has a life of its own. What this means is that your child can be going through a quiet period when they are feeling relatively good. Then something happens, and it triggers intense, and perhaps unexpected, feelings of pet grief.

Normal Verbal Behaviors

- Talking about their deceased pet a lot

- Talking about the death itself

- Not discussing their pet or the death at all

- Acting like everything is okay in the beginning

- Asking many questions about what is happening or happened

- Or not asking any questions in the beginning

- Asking to be with the pet that died (doesn't mean the child is suicidal—don't ignore the possibility either)

- Engaging attention by talking a lot

- Saying silly things and acting out

- Sharing that they dreamt about their pet

- Talking about the fact they "felt," "heard," or "saw" their pet that died

- Sharing that they are afraid of things they weren't afraid of before

- Telling you that they are worried about other pets and other people dying or getting sick

Normal Emotional Behaviors

- Lots and lots of tears

- Crying when you don't expect it

- Inflated feeling about seemingly small issues

- Over-reacting to an issue, comment, or event

- Not able to concentrate or focus

- Non-cooperation towards you and other adults

- Needing to be near you or another adult all the time

- Being overly angry with everyone and the situation

- Seeing a live pet and believing it is the pet that died

- Forgetful

- Lower self-esteem

- Irritability

- Acting out, such as clowning

- Creating more activities with the pet (if the pet is in the dying process)

Normal Physical Behaviors

- Eating more

- Not eating

- Sleeping more than usual

- Not sleeping

- Urine or bowel accidents

- New pain in the stomach and other areas undiagnosed by doctor

- Recurrent illnesses, such as colds, sore throats, and headaches

- An older child regressing: clinging, wanting to do babyish things, such as suck a bottle, play with dolls, suck thumb

- Hitting, biting, pinching, and other aggressive behaviors

- Needing to touch people more

- Being very tired, weary, and fatigued, even with enough sleep

- Wanting to destroy things

I am here to tell you to let this happen to your child. Let them feel what they are going through with you as a guide. Their pet meant a lot to them. Let those feelings of sadness happen and let their tears flow. It's healthy and necessary.

Yet, if your child is experiencing any abnormal grief feelings, then it's time to seek professional help from your physician or other health care professional trained to support a child through such behaviors.

Abnormal Grief Feelings and Behaviors

- Risk-taking that is dangerous

- Hurting themselves via self-destructive behaviors

- Threatening to hurt themselves, others, and/or other living pets/animals

- Play that is violent

- Withdrawal from people and animals, especially any living family pets

- A dramatic change in personality

- Inability to function

- Any normal behaviors that become extreme or are exhibited for a very long time

- Use of drugs or alcohol

- Wanting to die

- Inability to want to acknowledge the death of their pet over a period of time

With children they will experience the grief of their pet more sporadically than you or another adult. Even though their emotions may be more intense in the beginning, this will change as they age, develop, and experience life. When you supply a healthy grief model for your child—in later years when they are faced with illness, grief, and loss, they will be reminded of what they experienced in the past and make better choices for themselves.

Children can put grief aside much easier than adults. They will often focus for a time on more pleasant things. You read about this in the beginning of this chapter with Rebecca and Peter with their dog, Knox.

During this period, allow your child to have opportunities to express their grief, tell their stories, share their memories, and process what death means to them (chapters 11 to 14). During these times when they are expressing themselves, you may find the intense feelings come and go.

Keep in mind, grief has no time limit and will come and go throughout your child's life. If you allow and encourage your child to openly share their feelings about the illness or death of their pet, it will normalize this experience for them in the future.

Finally, you may also witness in your child a remarkable emotional growth spurt as a result of their pet loss. One of the results of going through grief—whether it be a child's grieving or an adult's—is personal growth. This will not lessen the sense of grief your child may experience or imply that the pet's illness or death was a good thing. Many of my clients have told me that their children have become more compassionate toward other people and animals, value more their friends and family members, especially living pets, and appreciate the life they had with their pet.

Chapter Wrap-Up

When your child's pet dies, it is extremely difficult. Their pet may have been their confidant and constant companion, offering them many moments of learning, love, and attention. The first 24 hours will probably be one of the most difficult transitions for them to experience.

Try to understand not only their feelings but also your unique feelings of grief. Spend time just being in the moment with your child by breathing and preparing yourself for the journey to come. Revisit the normal behaviors and feelings related to grief in this chapter and review the adult feelings of grief list (there's a link to this article in the "Resources" section of this book).

In chapter 7 I am going to teach you the seven stages of grief that your child may or may not experience in full. With each of these stages, I am going to give you examples of what you can expect from your child.

Tidbits of Wisdom

1. *Spend time today observing your grieving child as they simply "be."*

2. *When your child cries, resist the urge to encourage them to stop. Instead, hold them gently and let the crying continue as long and as hard as your child wants.*

3. *Reassuring your child that their feelings are okay is the perfect gift from your heart to theirs.*

7. Stages of Grief

For your child, losing a beloved animal companion can be really tough as well as for the entire family. Most children will be able to adjust to the death of a pet if you support them with honesty, compassion, empathy, and simple answers to their questions. Yet even so—you still will be faced with challenges.

In this chapter, I am going to explain the seven stages of grief. For adults, these stages can be experienced simultaneously, in a different order, or some may be not experienced at all.

Keep in mind for children, on the other hand, the stages of grief may be less clear because of the difference in their development level and their comprehension of death. It differs from adults. However, never assume your child is too young or too old to grieve.

Since grief is a necessary process in life, know it will take time for you and your family to grieve in a healthy way. The death of a pet provides your child with the chance to learn about becoming a healthy adult.

To help your child grieve in a healthy way and for you to recognize what stage of grief they may be experiencing, it can be very helpful to explain death in a clear and honest way. For example, "Even though your pet died and you loved them, you are not separated by death. Your pet will never really go away because you have loving memories of them."

Dr. Elisabeth Kubler-Ross was a pioneer in the hospice movement. While she wasn't a pet grief person, what she discovered can be applied to the passage of pet grief for you and your child.

In 1969, in her book *On Death and Dying,* Dr. Kubler-Ross made the five steps of grief and/or death well-known. These five steps covered the stages of grieving for the death of a loved one:

1. Denial
2. Anger
3. Bargaining
4. Depression
5. Acceptance

These five stages became very popular and are referred to widely, mostly during the dying process of people. However, people in this field began to expand on her various philosophies and standards. Currently there are seven stages of grief:

1. Shock and Denial
2. Pain and Guilt
3. Anger and Bargaining
4. Depression, Reflection, and Loneliness
5. Adjustment to Life
6. New Normal
7. Acceptance and Hope

These are the seven stages of grief I refer to in my practice when helping people and their families explore their grief and loss stages in regard to pet illness and loss. Many parents tell me that even though children process grief at a different pace, knowing this valuable information has helped the parents with their own grief with the death of a family pet. These stages of grief will guide you to a deeper understanding of what you are experiencing, what your child is experiencing, and how you can help them in a healthy and compassionate way.

Keep in mind since this journey is not only your child's as it is also your journey, your child may not experience the stages of grief as you do. Yet, they may. The more knowledge you have, the more effective and supportive you will be.

Whatever your child's experience, keep in mind it is normal and natural, so be compassionate with them about what they and possibly other family members are going through. Never compare their experience to their brother or sister's grief experience—grief isn't experienced in exactly the same way by all children. It is a unique and special journey they are undergoing according to the relationship they had with the pet, their age, and maturity.

Case Study—Emma, Gracie, and the Seven Stages

Lynn called me when her daughter, Emma's dog, Gracie, was diagnosed with cancer. They worked with me during that time and in the first few months after Gracie died. Lynn wanted step-by-step help and guidance to support her child with a healthy grief experience. Emma, ten at the time, was extremely mature and well-adjusted. Her mom and dad provided her with a very balanced and healthy life.

Since Emma was very mature for her age, she actually did experience all seven stages of grief. Not only that, but also she experienced all seven stages in order. They were not at the same intensity, but Emma still had hints of each stage of grief.

Please keep in mind Emma already had a healthy grasp on what death meant because Gracie had been sick for a long time. When Emma first received news her dog had cancer, it was hard for her to believe it was really true.

Stage One: Shock and Denial

Initially in our work together, Emma did not believe that Gracie was truly sick and instead believed that it was really not happening. Emma was faced with more than she could handle, and, as children do, she stepped out of her real world and into one that was more acceptable to her. She began to block out the unpleasant news of Gracie's sickness. Even though this was normal to do in the beginning of her journey, Lynn and her husband, Chip, began to provide Emma with more and more factual information that was well paced with what she could understand in accordance with her age and with her shock concerning Emma's imminent death.

Stage Two: Pain and Guilt

After Gracie's death, for a very short time, Emma suffered from pain and guilt. She felt she hadn't told Gracie she'd loved her often enough, was overwhelmed she had been reluctant or slow to feed Gracie on some days and had depended on her parents instead.

Luckily, this was a short stage for Emma. If the situation is overwhelming, these feelings of pain and guilt can become deep secrets that children do not share with anyone. Some behaviors you might notice are they appear depressed or unusually good-natured. They may also blame someone else for their pet's death.

Stage Three: Anger and Bargaining

Later, Emma's grief came out as anger, which is a very common emotion for children. She got angry with herself, her friends, and her parents. She was acting out with disruptive behavior when playing with her friends. Lynn even heard Emma asking her best friend if she could help her bring Gracie back to life by promising they would be friends forever.

Since Emma's emotions were generated by the grief she felt, Emma believed her feelings were powerful (though confusing). Unlike adults, children don't often understand how to deal with these emotions. At the age of ten Emma had not yet learned how to identify, separate, and fully express what was going on.

What Emma was asking for at this time was for her parents to fix and return her life to the way it had been before Gracie had died. She even asked them if she made her bed every day whether Gracie could come back to life.

Stage Four: Depression, Reflection, and Loneliness

Depression in a child after their pet dies is very common, and you can expect this if their pet was very special to them. Watch your child's behavior to notice if they are tired all the time, complain of not feeling well, have poor concentration, and have episodes of withdrawal. If you observed these behaviors and other forms of grief we discussed in chapter 6, keep a dialogue open with your child to lovingly support them.

When Emma began to display periods of depression, it began with her not wanting to go over to her best friend's house. She instead stayed home and started to be more preoccupied with Gracie's death. She started to not eat, hide her feelings of anger, and cry more often.

If you notice the depression intensifies or goes on for a long period of time with your child, seek professional help and stay in touch with their teacher or school counselor if appropriate.

Lynn and Chip provided Emma with many coping techniques to help her during the depression. They found the one that really worked was to encourage Emma to draw her favorite memories about Gracie—since Emma loved to draw.

Stage Five: Adjustment to Life

When Gracie first died, Lynn and Chip felt it was a good idea to let Emma stay home from school. They'd talked about this with Emma before Gracie was euthanized (chapter 10), and Emma had agreed it was a good idea.

However, Lynn and Chip found that after three days, Emma wanted to get back to school as soon as she could. It was a big part of her life and her friends were there. Lynn and Chip felt that was a great sign for Emma. Returning to school was a sign for Emma that life does continue even after death, something they'd talked a lot about before Gracie died.

The routine of school, which Emma loved, helped her with feeling secure, which is a feeling that can get lost with grief and death.

Stage Six: Your Child's New Normal

As time moved on, Emma began to adjust to the changes. In the days right after Gracie's euthanasia, Emma thought her life had changed permanently for the worse. However, because her parents had been working through their own beliefs on death and grieving, they were able to help Emma adjust.

This period of change and adjustment from life with the family pet to a new life without them—a new normal—will be a challenge both you and your child will go through together.

Stage Seven: Acceptance and Hope

When Emma began to experience the last stage of pet grief, she was ready to move forward with an entirely different attitude. She accepted the fact Gracie had died.

Her questions had been answered honestly by her parents. She processed her emotions and physical reactions with art projects, designed a funeral for Gracie (chapter 12), and wrote a beautiful tribute thanking Gracie for being her best friend.

Her experience, although difficult, was a beautiful and life-changing one. Lynn and Chip provided so much support, patience, and guidance for Emma. They helped Emma go to school, be with her friends, and understand death is not something to be afraid of.

When I last spoke with Emma, she told me she decided to write and illustrate a book that would help other children that had a dog that died, and she hoped it would help a lot of girls and boys her age.

Chapter Wrap-Up

The seven stages of grief provide references to guide you on how you can process your feelings of grief as well as support your child and family when the family pet has died. Emma experienced all seven stages in the exact order—and had lots of support from her parents. Your child by no means needs to experience all seven stages of grief or experience them in the exact order as Emma did. The important thing is for you to support and guide them through their particular grief experience.

In the next chapter I am going to teach you about the myths that surround pet grief and how these myths can hold your child back from healing grief and loss. I am also going to show you how to turn these myths around, so you can help your child with their journey.

Tidbits of Wisdom

1. *Honor the stage of grief that your child is in. Let them move at their own pace.*

2. *Stages of grief are more common for adults, yet they are still normal for your child, depending on their age and maturity level.*

3. *There is no rush when you child's pet dies to make things better. Instead, take a breath and be aware of the teaching moments.*

8. Myths about How Children Grieve

Now that you have an understanding of what constitutes normal grief for a child (chapter 6) and have explored the seven stages of grief (chapter 7) that a child may or may not fully experience, you are hopefully beginning to recognize what your child may be going through. Along with grief, there are a multitude of myths that come along with how children supposedly express their emotions with the illness and/or death of a pet.

It is important to consider how these myths will affect your child as they experience their journey. We have many pre-conceived ideas as to what death is about—how we and our children "should" react to it, avoid it, or dread it. No matter where you are with your beliefs, it is important to approach these myths with an openness and willingness to help your child.

Since the myths are a little different for children than adults, I have included a link in the "Resources" section of this book to articles I wrote about "adult" myths to help guide you through your own grief so you can be prepared for what your child may be exposed to.

To introduce the myths, let's explore the experience of Phoebe, a child whom I supported in her grief journey after the loss of her beloved tuxedo cat, Piroette.

Helping Phoebe and Piroette

Phoebe's mom and dad were very concerned with wanting to be totally honest with Phoebe about the death of her cat, Piroette. On our fourth call, they told me they were getting confused by some of the things they were reading online. They were getting conflicting information, and most of the information was geared towards adults.

In order for Phoebe's mom and dad to be able to help Phoebe cope with the loss, they wanted clarity, so Phoebe could have the same understanding and support that is offered to adults in grieving and mourning the death of a pet.

Initially in sharing their story, Phoebe's parents were overwhelmed. They wanted to do the best they could for Phoebe but didn't know where to begin. They knew they wanted to be honest, compassionate, and create a safe place for Phoebe to express what she was going through.

My response to Phoebe's parents was to first go over the adult grief myths, help them discover their own feelings around grief and dying, and then address the myths on how children grieve.

With my guidance, they permitted themselves to experience a range of feelings and to try to understand how they, themselves, felt, and from there to decide how they were going to communicate with and help Phoebe. They realized patience was going to be extremely critical for them to help their daughter and there was no single way to lovingly support Phoebe when coping with the loss of Piroette.

While Phoebe's parents were working with me, they developed wonderful and helpful ways to support Phoebe that would also make sense to Phoebe. They had an entire toolbox filled with ideas they could produce quickly if Phoebe was having a difficult time, such as art, plays, crafts, and memory projects (chapter 5). In this way they supported Phoebe so she could experience death in a very healthy, loving, and positive way.

Myths about grieving, like the ones that Phoebe's parents shared with me, have been around for a long time, and they can either really help or be a hindrance to your child's healing process. The key to making these myths help your child is to be aware of them, know how you feel about them, and then learn the truth.

The Myths about How Children Grieve

1. *Children don't grieve.*

Truth—Children will suffer and sometimes very acutely. It will depend on the situation and the personality of your child. The Harvard Child Bereavement Study conducted by William Worden and Phyllis Silverman showed that even with all the research available that proves children do grieve, myths and misunderstanding still persist about the impact grief has on children.

The fact that the myth—children don't grieve or children are too young to grieve—is still very prevalent greatly disserves our children. One simple disservice is this myth, if believed, will deprive your child of the ability to grieve. Therefore, they'll be forced to stuff their feelings in.

The studies conducted by Jana DeCristofaro, LCSW, coordinator of children's grief services at The Dougy Center, The National Center for Grieving Children and Families, found infants grieve as well. DeCristofaro stated in one of her studies, "[Infants] will know that the person who is holding them does not smell the same, feel the same, or carry them in the same way."

Even though Phoebe was ten years old, she grieved every night when she could not cuddle Piroette while reading her book. Her stuffed animals, even though she loved them, were not the same. Phoebe's experience undoubtedly defied this myth.

2. *Children grieve the same way adults do.*

Truth—Since grief happens with children, they do in fact grieve in similar ways to adults. Yet, they also experience and express their grief differently.

In my practice, I have experienced that children tend to grieve for shorter periods of time. It is difficult for them to have sadness, anger, or cry for longer, sustained periods of time, which is what I see more commonly with adults.

It is almost as if children can jump in and out of grief. This can give a parent, like Phoebe's parents, the false belief that their child is coping well. However, the jumping in and out could be a way that children distract themselves. This behavior allows children to better handle the force of the intense emotions brought on by the illness or death of their pet.

Depending on their age, feelings of personal grief, or stage of grief, a child is constantly moving from one emotion to the next. When you are aware of your own and their feelings, it can offer you a wonderful experience of bonding with your child, especially if you have some activities for you and your child to express yourselves.

3. *Grief happens in a nice and neat package.*

Truth—As with following the seven stages of grief in chronological order (chapter 7), the same is true about your child's unique grief experience—meaning there is not a single or perfect or correct experience for them. As with adults, a child will have their own process and ways of grieving.

There are so many factors to consider that will influence the reactions of your child. Besides age, temperament, and personality of your child, their behavior and grief experiences will depend on the relationship they had with their pet, the pet's manner of death, and the reaction that you and other adults show.

4. *Grief in a child is always visible.*

Truth—As adults we have been taught that in order to be strong and independent we should not show our grief. It may burden others, and it is inappropriate to let other people know how we are feeling. Because of this we believe if children do not openly show they are grieving, they are not grieving at all.

When the death of a pet occurs, a child could be grieving tremendously on the inside. They go into shock and other forms of grief just like you do as an adult. However, it has been shown that children may not outwardly show intense grief early or even in the first year. It may take a few years or even show up years later in adulthood.

This shows that grieving in children depends on their development. Susan Thomas, LCSW-R, director of the Center for HOPE, found that as children age and develop more skills, they will oftentimes grieve again with the memories about the death of their pet. For example, a child's dog dies when the child is eight years old. Then, they don't get another dog until they are in their twenties. Grief from the first experience can resurface when they get the new dog even though it is years later.

Children have a wide range of emotions just as adults do, and it may not always be possible for you to know if your child is feeling sad. By knowing what normal and abnormal grief can look like for children (chapter 6 and 7), you will become better able to recognize and help them cope with their grief.

5. *Silence is golden.*

Truth—In general our society teaches that verbally expressing grief feelings can be a sign of weakness, especially grief in regard to the deaths of animals. Your child may not want to verbalize what they are feeling because they are taking cues from the adults around them.

Since children are extremely perceptive, they may notice or even fear to bring up the fact they miss their pet because they will cause more sadness and tears.

If children are encouraged to stay silent and not have the freedom to express themselves, they can create a myriad of false beliefs in their own minds—guilt that they somehow caused their pet to die; the belief that if they had behaved better, their pet would still be alive; or even the belief that they could have done something to prevent their pet from dying.

Since it is important for children to feel comfortable, loved, and safe when expressing themselves, it is not helpful to force them to talk. Let them process their grief with your gentle support.

6. *Grief will go away someday.*

Truth—As with adults, grief never goes away! There is no timeline. As an adult you may be able to come to terms with the loss, but children don't really do so until they are in their mid-to late-twenties. They need time to grieve, mourn (chapter 11), and adjust to the change.

Since this process lasts a lifetime, you can see the importance of the role pets can play in explaining illness, grief, and death. The loss of a pet gives you the opportunity to not treat death as something to be fixed. Instead you are given the opportunity to provide a way to support your child in coping with life's stages by providing love, compassion, and honesty.

7. *Don't tell your child the truth about death.*

Truth—As an adult you may believe children are better off not knowing about or talking about the fact their pet died. You may instead choose to create many stories around this event that are not true.

The fact is, children can handle the truth. When you don't tell children the truth, it actually does not protect them from grief; it only leaves them to grieve alone according to Andy McNiel, MA, CEO of the National Alliance for Grieving Children.

If your child is young and you tell them their pet "got lost," "went to sleep," "expired," or "ran away," it could be very confusing and evening isolating for them, rather than helpful (chapter 9).

According to McNiel, truth is preferable to lying. Lying fosters mistrust. Clear language helps children develop a healthy and normal view surrounding death. Using concrete language will help a child be less fearful. It is healthiest to say, "Pirouette's heart stopped, she doesn't breathe anymore, and you won't see her again." This may feel heartless and painful to share with a child, but when you are truthful, you will be developing a deeper long-term trust with your child to have open dialogue not only about death but about other life events as well.

8. *Rituals are for adults only.*

Truth—Some of my parents are concerned about allowing their children to create or attend a burial or funeral for their pet (chapter 13). They think such rituals are for adults and could possibly be harmful for children—or, at the very least, not interesting or relevant. This is a very common myth.

Children are capable of participating in the creation of a ritual for their pet. Like the truths with the myths above—if we allow children to process their grief in ways that are appropriate for them, it will open the dialogue and provide for a stronger bond among family members.

Some things to keep in mind—your child should:

- Not be forced to create a funeral or other ritual

- Be encouraged to create a ritual that is meaningful for them

- Be able to leave the ritual with your support if it becomes overwhelming

The Other Side of the Myths: Grace and Compassion

These myths are very common, and many parents think they are true. These myths can easily trigger your grief or your child's. If you are not aware of the myths, you may become confused as to why your child is suddenly feeling sad or very angry.

Even though it may be a well-meaning teacher, friend, or family member, when one of them offers your child a myth as a so-called "word of wisdom," it can trigger pet loss grief in your child. However, once you become aware of these myths and why they are not true, you will be able to react to them and help your child with grace and compassion.

Here is the thing about believing these myths and letting them affect your decisions—I have seen in my practice when folks believe and live by these myths, their children get stuck in their grief and have a very difficult time.

When parents learn to familiarize themselves with these myths, debunk them, and replace them with positive thoughts and actions, they are able to spend more time helping their children navigate their feelings to emerge more emotionally strong and healthy.

Please read my articles on the myths that adults experience, a link to which you can find in the "Resources" section of this book. These articles will help you be prepared for the multitude of thoughts and feelings that you will have, and the comments people will make to you so you can learn to be more present for your child—and yourself.

Chapter Wrap-Up

The illness and death of a child's pet is one of the most complete learning experiences that they will encounter. Many aspects of their being will be challenged to develop, like the emotional, spiritual, behavioral, physical, and cognitive parts of themselves. Some children will be able to adjust and grieve over the loss of their pet, but others may have more challenges.

As children age and develop, it is important to help them grieve with every stage. Behavioral issues may develop in a cumulative way that lend to confusion, pain, anxiety, and other emotions that will not be understood until they approach adulthood.

Myths about pet loss grief can be roadblocks to moving forward with meaning and purpose in regard to the bond you have with your child and the bond they have with their pet. The way to remove the roadblocks and make the myths work for you and your child is to be aware of them, debunk them, and then replace them with something positive.

To repeat, always remember—you and your child are not alone in your grief journey. There are others that are experiencing the same thing. Find those people and spend time with them.

In chapter 9 I am going to help you prepare and deliver the truth to your child with even more detail about how to do so. When your child's pet dies, this will be your opportunity to offer them loving and positive support. You will continue to learn why creating myths could negatively affect them in their adult years.

Tidbits of Wisdom

1. *Shedding myths surrounding the death of your child's pet will give you and your child life.*

2. *Honesty does not create a myth. Honesty creates truth, and our children and pets expect that from us.*

3. *When myths trigger grief, it gives a way for honest, open dialogue with your child when sharing stories about their pet.*

9. Telling Children the Truth

When your child's pet dies, this will be your opportunity for an optimal yet loving teaching moment. Instead of creating myths that could affect them into their adult years—telling the truth and encouraging and answering their questions gives you the opportunity to build a compassionate bond and deep trust.

Something to keep in mind when answering their questions is to be specific, straightforward, and brief. This doesn't mean you will be cold or harsh—in fact, it is the opposite. By keeping your answers clear and concise, you are meeting your child at their stage of development, which shows great respect.

Plus, be sure your answers are at the age and development level of your child. Understand that it is okay for you to say you don't know the answer, instead of creating a myth (chapter 8), which can inhibit their process of understanding, grieving, healing, and gaining emotional depth.

Since children absorb only bits of information at a time, it is important as a parent to pay attention to their body language, facial expressions, and signs that they are done with your answer for the moment. One way to recognize this is they will continue to ask you the same question over again a few times to be able to comprehend what you are sharing.

Patience at this point is critical. The last thing you would want to do is shut down a potentially great moment of teaching and love.

In this chapter I am going to go over some of the common questions you may encounter and how you can answer them. You will hear how Jenny helped her daughter Sara (age 6) when explaining the death of Sara's guinea pig, Miss Piggy. I will also include suggestions for talking with older children.

Common Questions

When you get the news your child's pet is going to die or has already died, the first thing to do is stay attuned to your child's reactions to see if they understand what you are saying. If you are not sure what your child means when they ask a question, it is okay to ask them more about what they meant or even what they know about grief and dying.

Let's explore how Jenny answered Sara's questions about the death of her pet guinea pig, Miss Piggy.

Q: Why Did Miss Piggy Die?

A: The thing to consider first is why are they asking this question. Is it because your child may feel sad, angry, or even guilty about the animal's sickness or death? If this is the case it is important to allow your child to tell you what they are thinking and feeling. However, they may also be asking about the actual process of death.

With Sara it was a physical experience and question. Jenny handled it by answering in the following way, "Miss Piggy died because her body just stopped working. She stopped eating, moving, seeing, and hearing. We are going to all miss her."

If your child is older, you could say, "Miss Piggy's body hurts, and she is very old. She has trouble eating, so she is not getting the nutrients she needs. Remember how I explained to you that the body needs food and water to be healthy?"

Q: When Is Miss Piggy Coming Back?

A: Jenny told Sara in a very beautiful, gentle, and loving way that when things die, they do not come back. Here is what she said, "Sara, as much as you loved Miss Piggy and as much as you want her to come back to you, she can't because she has died. You can still feel love and have your memories about all the fun things you did with Miss Piggy. Miss Piggy will always be special to you."

With an older child you can explain in more detail the process of death. Just always keep in mind the reaction of your child.

For example, you could add to Jenny's words, "All living things die and that doesn't mean you did anything wrong. It is just the nature of the cycle of life." Always try to keep your answers short and allow your child to probe for more information.

Q: Where Is Miss Piggy Now?

A: The first thing I guide my clients to find out before they answer this question is where their child thinks their pet is. Your response would then be tailored on that belief. Plus, your response will be according to your spiritual or religious belief. The older the child, the more detail about burial, cremation, and spiritual or religious events you will be able to share.

In Jenny's case Sara believed Miss Piggy went to heaven because that is the family's religious belief. Jenny validated that by sharing, "Yes, Sara, Miss Piggy went to heaven with all the other animals that were loved by their families."

If your family is more spiritual in nature, like many of my clients are, you can tell your child that there is a special part of their pet that exists after the body dies. This part is called the soul or spirit. The soul or spirit is not a part of the body, but rather is the part of their pet that makes them special.

All over the world, people believe that the soul or spirit lives on in our memories and hearts, so in that a way, their pet that died is always with them.

Q: Will You Die Too?

A: This question is probably the toughest. It will inspire and test your ability to be honest with your child. Having a pet so that your child can explore this question as they develop into adulthood is paramount.

It is important when answering this question to give lots of compassion, love, reassurance, support, and HONESTY.

Jenny replied to Sara, "I will die sometime, but I hope to be here a long time. I am healthy, and I am not sick."

Since Sara was afraid of losing her mom and the death of Miss Piggy triggered this fear, Jenny asked a clarifying question, "Are you worried that I won't be here to take care of you?"

Of course, you will base the answers to these questions according to the age of your child. My clients struggle with their answers to this most difficult question, and it is best if you have some answers already prepared, as this is a very common question. Everyone has a different answer to this question, depending on their belief system.

The one thing that is to be expected—your child will need another level of love and understanding. Reassurance with honesty is paramount. Answering them with, "I will never die and leave you alone" will create a myth, so avoid such a response.

Q: How Long Will I Live?

A: Again here is a perfect example of how animals can teach children about death, dying, and grief.

Jenny explained to Sara when she was asking about what happened to Miss Piggy, "No one knows how long they will live, Sara, and no living being lives forever." She continued to assure Sara that most people and even some animals live for a long time.

Jenny also focused on life. I had her ask Sara, "What is life?" She encouraged Sara to say things about what life is. Jenny started by giving Sara her own examples of what life is: "I am breathing, and I am alive. I can hear, and I am alive." Soon after doing this, Sara started to add her own "I am alive" statements.

If your child is older, the above exercise is still very useful. Additionally, this would be the perfect time to give them a more detailed account of the process of illness and death, always keeping in mind how much they can assimilate and where they are in their stage of grief (chapters 3, 4, and 7).

Chapter Wrap-Up

Being honest with your child when their pet is faced with illness or has died is your opportunity to support them with compassion, reassurance, and clarity.

It may seem easier to answer their questions by hiding the truth from them or not letting them experience this very necessary learning. Yet, by including a pet in your child's life and having them experience this part of the cycle of life, you have the opportunity to build a compassionate bond and deep trust with your child.

This is not an easy time, and it will demand that you stay present with your child. It will change your child's life and how they experience the world around them. Prepare yourself by revisiting the questions from this chapter, begin to internalize them, and determine your own answers to help you build a trusting bond of compassion with your child.

In the next chapter you will learn the guidelines for supporting your child with the concept of euthanasia or with the news of their pet's sudden death. Since this is such a difficult decision as an adult to make, explaining it to your child can be a challenge. Knowing how you feel is the first step.

Tidbits of Wisdom

1. *Telling the truth to your child about the death of their pet is loving and compassionate. Feel that in your heart as you answer their questions.*

2. *Truth is an exercise of staying present in the moment. Nothing else.*

3. *Love is truth and does not die. Truth is constant and works well when explaining death.*

10. Explaining Euthanasia or Sudden Death

Neglecting or avoiding discussing the concepts of euthanasia and sudden death to children is not uncommon. As adults it can be extremely difficult to make such a difficult decision ourselves for our pets, so to be able to explain euthanasia or the news that your child's pet got hit by a car can be a challenge.

As mentioned already, it important for you to know and embrace how you are feeling too. Having compassion and understanding for what you are experiencing first will give you the strength and loving ability to deliver this difficult news to your child with compassionate honesty.

When you can be as honest as possible when explaining euthanasia or sudden death to your child, the impact in the long run will be less traumatic. If you try to protect your child from these potentially traumatic end-of-life issues, grief, and loss—you will unfortunately miss a trust-building opportunity to teach your child in a healthy, loving, and non-scary way.

There are honest yet extremely loving ways to share with your son and/or daughter many end-of-life issues that are age-appropriate to help them understand and accept the fact that it is time to help their pet die or that their pet died suddenly.

I had one client who was 51 years old before her mother told her the honest truth about her childhood cat. Her mom and dad had told her, when she was a child, that her cat had gone to live with her aunt whom she'd never met—all the way across the county—when actually her cat was euthanized when she was at school. When she finally found out as a 51-year-old adult, she was angry and her heart was wounded with grief that her parents hadn't told her the truth. It took her a lot of work to forgive her mother and father.

As we have talked about in this book, pet loss can be very traumatic to a child. The relationship they had with their pet, their age, and maturity level (chapter 4) all should be considered. Whether they had a dog, cat, goldfish, or bird, this relationship gave them companionship, love, confidence, and a built-in playmate. When their pet dies, this experience can leave them with many feelings of grief, such as anger, distrust, loneliness, anxiety, insecurity, and fear.

When you respect what their pet meant to them and consider their age and their understanding of death—you can help them experience healthy grief by carefully planning how you are going to teach them about their pet's euthanasia or sudden death.

To learn how you can best teach your child about euthanasia or sudden death,

I am going to share the story of Simon, Noelle, and their 11-year-old daughter, Logan. They worked with me to help Logan cope when Destiny, Logan's rabbit, needed to be euthanized. From these recommendations, you can find guidance for informing and supporting your child.

Recommendations for Helping Your Child Cope with a Pet's Sudden Death or Euthanasia

1. Be accessible, truthful, and honest.

The most important thing here is to tell your child as soon as possible when you find out that euthanasia is necessary and pending. You do not want them to hear it from someone else—as you will not have control of what others will say.

I shared with Simon and Noelle to tell Logan the truth from the beginning. This way they will grow a trusting bond with her now and in the future. They understood if they weren't truthful with Logan, she might discover they distorted the truth or lied to her. They understood Logan's trust in them in the future would be compromised.

2. Give your child basic, age-and maturity-level-appropriate explanations to their questions.

A child's grief is normal and necessary, and it is okay for them to feel sad. Simon and Noelle reassured Logan many times by saying, "Logan, it is okay to feel sad that Destiny died. This is how it is supposed to feel when someone we love dies."

I explained to Simon and Noelle to avoid using the phrase "put to sleep" as it could give Logan anxiety over her own sleeping. A child shouldn't think death is the same as sleeping. Here is what Simon and Noelle said to Logan, "When you and I sleep, our body is still working. It is just resting."

Also it is important to avoid the terms "passed away" or "left you." Since these terms could imply their pet left temporarily or abandoned the child, these words might encourage them to hope unrealistically for their pet's return.

3. Help them understand why euthanasia is necessary.

Old age—To help Logan understand why euthanasia was needed, Simon and Noelle explained that Destiny was suffering from old age. They explained, "Logan, Destiny was a very old rabbit. You took excellent care of her, and she won many awards for you in 4-H. But Destiny was old, and her body stopped working."

Chronic illness—If your child's pet is suffering from a terminal illness, you can explain to your child, "Because the disease can't be cured or stopped, your pet is very sick. Their body has stopped working."

Sudden death—An accident that happened to your child's pet can be a challenge to explain with the truth. As difficult as it might seem, you can tell them, "A horrible thing happened to your pet's body. It was hit by a car [for example] and was badly hurt. Your pet could not be fixed, and their body stopped working."

4. Avoid telling your child that God or another Spiritual Deity wanted the animal to be in Heaven/Universe with them or with a relative and/or another pet that had already died.

Children can easily become angry with God or the Spiritual Deity of your family's belief. They can develop a fear they will be chosen next by God or the Spiritual Deity to die. So, it is best to avoid saying anything on these lines.

5. Do not euthanize their pet without telling them first.

Simon and Noelle included Logan in the decision because doing so helps children better understand why the decision has to be made.

Simon and Noelle told me that when they asked Logan about her opinion on the euthanasia, she responded, "I am going to make sure I say goodbye to Destiny and tell her how much I love her." This gave Logan a sense of closure and a firm understanding that Destiny would not be in her physical life.

6. Involve them at the time of euthanasia.

Depending on your child's age and your personal choice, this experience can provide them with the reality of a peaceful death rather than creating a fantasy. Logan was 11 years old. She wanted to be present when the veterinarian came. This was Logan's first experience with euthanasia. Being present helped Logan by removing the mystery and keeping any fear from developing into a negative memory.

Chapter Wrap-Up

When explaining euthanasia or sudden death to your child, you can see how difficult it can be. Yet it is extremely important to explain and include your child with decisions and discussions surrounding this event.

This experience gives you, the parent, the opportunity to communicate to your child what euthanasia is and why it is necessary. It also gives you another chance to have compassion for yourself as a parent, especially if your heart is breaking as well at the loss of a family pet.

It may seem heartless and maybe even cruel to be honest with your child about this difficult choice, yet, as you can see from Simon and Noelle, they supported Logan with honesty and love about the euthanasia of Destiny, which, in turn, helped Logan cope better.

After one year had passed, they called to tell me that when Logan talks about her experience of being at Destiny's euthanasia, she describes it in a very positive and honest way. This honesty built normality, depth, and trust into Logan's emotional development.

Like Simon and Noelle, you can share with your child honest yet extremely loving ways to explain the end-of-life issues, all the while making sure to be age-appropriate. This will help them understand and accept the fact that it is time to help their pet die or that their pet died suddenly with dignity, respect, and love.

In the next chapter you are going to begin to learn ways to support and help your child through the mourning process. You will discover that grief is different than mourning and how important it is for your child to mourn the loss of their pet. I am going to share the ways in which I support my clients to express mourning with their children.

Tidbits of Wisdom

1. *The choice of euthanasia encourages support, love, and compassion with your child when you allow them to participate in the decision.*

2. *Honesty with end-of-life issues prepares your child for reality rather than fantasy.*

3. *The euthanasia of a pet can be experienced as a sign of love and responsible caretaking for an old, sick, or injured pet.*

CELEBRATION OF YOUR CHILD'S PET: SECTION THREE

Even if we're apart . . . I'll always be with you.

—Winnie the Pooh

11. A Child's Experience of Mourning

For many of us, the words "grief" and "mourning" have been used interchangeably to mean the same thing. However, they are quite different. Knowing that difference will help you to support your child with their journey of healing the grief over losing their animal companion.

Briefly, grieving is the *inward* expression of your child's emotions, and mourning is the *outward* expression of these emotions. Art projects, funerals, life celebrations, letter writing, and drawing (chapters 12 and 13) can be healthy expressions of mourning.

As you learned in chapters 6 and 7, grief is your child's emotional reaction or physical response to the death of their pet. Grief can be experienced as shock, confusion, anger, depression, sadness, anxiety, and more.

So many times in our society we forget to allow not only ourselves to mourn but our children as well. If you allow your child the opportunity to feel and express their grief, you will be accepting the fact that grief is normal for them. Their journey as they grow into being healthy adults will be greatly supported by you, and they will remember that.

Allowing them to express their grief outwardly through mourning allows their body, mind, and soul to deal with an event. They may not be able to fully process all their feelings in a particular moment. It takes time for them to grow and process their grief, so please be patient with them.

If the death of their pet was sudden or totally unexpected, their experience may take some time to completely understand. Conversely, if their pet was ill and suffering for a while, the time they need to process their grief may unfold quite differently.

The important thing to remember is that the loss of their pet is not entirely about losing their companion that they loved and shared life with. You should also take into consideration what dreams and experiences your child had with that pet, their age, and their development. For this reason, it is crucial that you give them "permission" to feel their loss in ways that are appropriate for them and to mourn that loss.

Case Study—Olivia and Thirsty

Olivia's dad, Ethan, called me when he found that with the loss of Olivia's goldfish, Thirsty, Olivia was being very quiet about what had happened. Ethan told me, "She was burying her emotions even though we were encouraging her to express herself."

I explained to Ethan to not worry at this point that Olivia was quiet. The experience was new, but they could start by softly and gently encouraging her to draw pictures or engage in other forms of non-verbal expression (chapter 13).

Olivia then drew lots and lots of pictures of her goldfish. Her father told me that over the course of two weeks, she drew twelve pictures, "They were so beautiful and colorful. They showed how much Olivia loved Thirsty. She even had little sayings about how she loved Thirsty on some of them. My partner and I took her drawings and made them into a book. This opened Olivia up, and she brought her book to show everyone at school. It was beautiful."

A Child's Mourning Experience

Keep in mind as you read this chapter that children oftentimes mourn more through physical behaviors rather than words. They will act them out and not be able to find words that describe how they are feeling.

1. Give your child time to accept that death is real.

Once a child understands that the pet that they loved is dead and will not be physically with them, they begin to accept that death is real. But, as mentioned previously, they will deal with that truth in doses. They let themselves express a little grief here and there, but then they may distract themselves by doing something else, like calling a friend or going out to play. Allowing your child to mourn in this way will help them understand how and why their pet died. Teaching your child when they are young will help your child as they get older to mourn in a healthy way.

2. Encourage them to embrace the pain.

As a child, they need to engage with the pain they are feeling regarding the loss. Most children are encouraged to stuff or deny their feelings. They are encouraged not to show the emotions of sadness or other feelings of grief. You can help your child by encouraging them to talk about the painful thoughts that make them sad about not having their pet with them. As a non-judgmental listener you can also share your feelings—staying aware of how they are reacting. Allowing your child to show their pain little by little is very healthy and loving. It will help them manage this loss as well as future losses in a healthy way.

3. Encourage your child to share memories of their pet.

When a pet dies, the pet will live in your child's heart forever. When your child is grieving and actively remembering their pet, they are celebrating the lessons they learned and how much their pet meant to them. This part of mourning is critical, so please do not feel the need to protect them or save them from their pain by not telling stories and sharing memories. It is healthy for a child to look at photos of their pet after they died and hear stories from others about their pet.

4. Help them to recognize their new normal.

Part of your child's identity was formed by the companionship they had with their pet. They interacted with their pet on a daily basis, so be aware of how your child has changed. Many times parents want to quickly replace the pet that died, so their child can avoid the painful learning or sensing of how they have changed or how they will live their daily life differently without their beloved companion. Encourage your child to outwardly express the new experience of living without their pet. In this way, you are providing them an outlet to actively and healthily process their grief.

5. Expect your child to ask questions—a lot of questions.

When your child's pet died, they may ask very simple questions as they are wondering about the meaning and purpose of life. "Why did my dog die?" and "What happened to Mac after he died?" are two of the most common I have come across in my practice.

When they ask these questions, they are outwardly mourning and seeking answers from adults they trust. Remember too, as we already discussed, if you don't know the answer to these questions, you can answer with "I don't know." It is critical you answer with truth and compassion.

6. Expect that mourning is ongoing.

Your child will need support throughout their development. Grief is a process that includes mourning. Your child, like you, will grieve and mourn long after the family pet has died. With compassionate, honest, and loving support your presence will be pivotal not only in the days and weeks following the death but in the months and years as they mature. As your child matures you can help them mourn each time on a deeper and more soulful level to help them grow to be a well-adjusted, healthy, and loving adult.

7. Encourage your child to design and perform a funeral or celebration.

Creating and performing a funeral or other life-affirming celebration for their pet (chapters 12 and 13) is healthy for you to encourage your child to do. Children oftentimes do not know what to expect with a funeral for a person. Having them create a funeral for their pet will teach them what to expect and lessen their fears. You can help them by explaining what is included in a funeral. Let them ask questions, as they will be curious. Creating and performing a funeral or other celebration is a powerful and healthy means for a child to engage with those grief emotions in order to mourn.

8. Help them choose a token.

After a pet has died, it is healing to ask a grieving child if they want to keep anything that was special to their pet as a way to remember them. For example, it could be a tuft of the pet's fur, a feather, a toy, a photo, or any object that represents their pet in a special way. This gives you the opportunity to help them open a dialogue as to why their pet was so important, especially if they are grieving quietly. Choosing a token is a wonderful way to have your child mourn because it allows a safe and calm place for your child to outwardly express themselves. A token is an item that your child will keep for many years.

9. Encourage "heart-connecting objects."

"Heart-connecting objects" are items your child takes comfort in that belonged to the pet that died. These objects can be leashes, toys, blankets, collars, or food bowls that offer your child a physical "heart connection" to the pet that died. Encourage them to carry around or hold the objects that they choose. Even if they want to take the item to bed or on family outings, allow that to happen—it is normal and natural for them to want to include their pet. This is a wonderful way to allow your child to mourn the loss when grieving is new, raw, and they are learning how to adjust.

10. Respect their relationship with their pet.

As you have learned throughout this book, your child will respond to the death of their pet in relation to the type of relationship that they had with their pet and in response to your reactions about the pet's death. The closer and more involved your child was with their pet, the more challenging their grief and mourning will be. The less the involvement will reflect that as well. However, funerals and life celebrations are still encouraged to teach children about different life events and to help them mourn in a positive, healthy way.

Chapter Wrap-Up

In this chapter you learned that both grief and mourning have different roles in your child's journey of healing the loss of their beloved companion. Even though they can overlap and have no timeframe, their outward expression of grief (i.e., mourning) will be an invaluable learning tool and a beautiful, sacred time for them and you.

In chapter 12 you will learn of actual ways to encourage your child to express their grief through some mourning rituals. When you and your child are ready to approach this step on the journey of losing your animal companion by holding a pet funeral, pet memorial, pet remembrance, and/or an end-of-life celebration, chapter 12 will guide you.

Tidbits of Wisdom

1. *A memory or a keepsake is significant for your child to mourn their pet. Encourage this with thought and seize the opportunity to openly dialogue.*

2. *Supporting an emotional connection between your child and their pet is paramount when mourning and healing.*

3. *The feelings and thoughts of your child as they mourn the loss of their pet are personal to them—and won't be the same as yours or those of other family members.*

12. Significance of a Pet Funeral and Other Mourning Rituals

The death of your child's pet may be the first time your child will experience the death of a loved one. Supporting and encouraging your child to outwardly celebrate the life they had with their companion can teach them how to manage all types of personal loss. This in itself is a valuable lesson for the rest of their lives.

Too often, I have seen in my practice that parents will sometimes be preoccupied with the logistics and their own emotions surrounding a family's pet. They forget to help their child grieve and mourn. I have also seen parents shield their child from death and funerals.

Since the subject of death is unfamiliar to children, it is up to you to teach and support them in a healthy way. My clients who help their children cope by telling them the truth (chapters 3 and 9) and creating some type of end-of-life celebration avoid having their children sense there is something wrong and possibly feel as if they are responsible for their pet's death.

As I have mentioned throughout this book, the grieving process for your child calls for guidance from you, so they can understand loss, mourn, and express themselves. Inviting your child to participate in decisions, such as burial, scattering the ashes, and planning a funeral, to the extent of your child's maturity and what you are comfortable with, will help them greatly.

When you are considering a pet funeral—know that children are naturally curious about death. Their age, maturity level, bond with their pet, and your behavior will all be influences.

In this chapter, you are going to learn the different ways in which you can support your child to both mourn and celebrate their pet's life—through a pet funeral or by creating another type of end-of-life celebration. In chapter 13 I will share with you ways in which your child can mourn by writing a love letter, and in chapter 5 you learned about creative ways through which children can feel safe with their feelings.

Since you are a very special parent that wants to honor your child and their pet, please remember that if someone says that you are weird for holding an end-of-life ceremony for a pet—PLEASE DON'T LISTEN! If you listen, you will be holding back a very important step for healing the grief of your family.

By supporting your child to experience the creative and necessary process of mourning (chapter 11) and exploring the options in this chapter, your child will have the chance to respectfully celebrate the life of their pet and thank them for everything they shared.

Also, by spending time allowing your child to create the end-of-life ceremony or by having a pet funeral celebrant help you create a personalized celebration, your child will get the chance to have some closure and say goodbye. I have been conducting pet funerals and pet memorials for many years, and I have found that holding a commemorative event is an invaluable aid in the healing process. I also love working with children with their creations because of their ability to be honest and innovative.

Allowing your child to express their feelings and pay tribute to their pet is healthy, normal, and essential.

How Liam and Emma Did It

My clients Liam and Emma hired me to help their daughter, Charlotte (age 9), create a beautiful celebration when her dog, Lily, was buried in their backyard. I met with Charlotte, Liam, and Emma on Skype, and helped Charlotte compose a beautiful eulogy that paid tribute to all the things that she'd shared with Lily.

Charlotte decided to invite not only her family, but also her friends that loved Lily as she had. Her parents told me when she read the eulogy, everyone was supportive of Charlotte by hugging her after she was finished reading.

After the ceremony Liam called and told me, "Wendy, the funeral that Charlotte created was absolutely perfect. I am so glad we had a funeral for Lily. It helped Charlotte so much."

Eulogy that Charlotte Wrote and Delivered about Lily

Hi, my name is Charlotte, and I would like to tell you how much I loved my dog, Lily.

Lily was my favorite dog in the entire world. She would follow me to the bus every day and helped me with my homework.

I loved her every single day, and I told her by hugging her and giving her a big kiss on the forehead.

Lily also liked it when I read to her before we went to sleep. Mom and Dad said it was okay to let Lily sleep in my bed, and I liked that because it was really fun.

Lily liked her toys, food, and sleeping with her legs sticking up in the air. That made me laugh.

I want to tell Lily that I am her best friend too and thank her for being mine.

I am happy all my friends are here.

Types of Celebrations

Here are some definitions of the types of end-of-life celebrations that you can consider when you are ready for this step in supporting your child with pet loss. I listed them here and will talk more about them later in this chapter.

Pet Funeral—This is a celebration/service in which the body or cremains of your child's pet are present. This event takes place relatively soon after the pet reaches the end of their life.

Pet Memorial—This is the celebration/service in which the body or cremains of your child's pet are not present. This event can take place whenever you and your child would like. There is no time limit as to when a pet memorial takes place.

Pet Remembrances—These are the anniversaries, holidays, and/or special occasions that your child shared with their pet during which you celebrate the memory of your child's pet.

Beneficial Outcomes for Your Child

The thing that I absolutely love about helping children and their parents plan and officiate a pet's funeral or memorial service is that I get to witness the unwavering amount of love and healing that takes place for not only that child but other family members as well.

Even though there is much sadness, there are moments of incredibly rich emotional sharing with the celebration of a pet's life. I witness life-changing events that children undergo by sharing their life with their cherished pet. I feel honored to be part of those tender moments shared by those who miss their pets and are mourning the loss of their treasured family member.

These are some of those life-changing moments that a pet funeral or memorial service can provide to support your child in their journey of healing pet loss grief.

A pet funeral, pet memorial, or pet remembrance can provide your child with:

- a sense of reality that their pet has reached the end of life;

- the opportunity for an honest and open dialogue that teaches them what a funeral is, what happens, etc.;

- preparation for human funerals in the future;

- a way to help them accept that death is part of life, depending on their age;

- a way for confirmation that death signifies that the pet is no longer living in the physical world but in a spiritual realm, depending on your spiritual beliefs;

- the opportunity for sharing thoughts, experiences, and feelings they had with their pet—as well as sharing by friends and family members;

- the space for them to acknowledge, reflect, and honor the incredible role that the animal played in their life—and for other participants to share as well; and/or

- a healthy way to say a formal goodbye.

A *pet funeral* is generally held within a few days of death and may consist of a viewing, a formal service, and a brief rite at the gravesite. The atmosphere is usually somber and sad, and the emphasis is on death, mourning, and loss.

The funeral can be held at a pet cemetery or in your backyard if your local ordinances allow this. Your child may invite family, friends, and even other pets that their pet loved. The ceremony you create can include music, the reading of a eulogy by your child that they wrote themselves, a celebration after the service, and time for others to share their feelings about your child's pet.

A *memorial service*, on the other hand, may be held at any time after the pet dies. Its function is to remember and celebrate the loved one's life. Oftentimes, the mood is more positive and uplifting. The service can be as small and private, or as open and elaborate, as you wish, and it can be delayed as long as its planning requires. Keep in mind, however, that having the service closer to the time when your child's loss is most deeply felt is when it is most likely to help your child, you, and your family express and work through grief.

Many of my clients who have chosen cremation choose a memorial service that includes spreading the ashes at a favorite locale that their child's pet loved. Many times a eulogy is also included or a celebration with food afterwards. Try to make it as comfortable as you can for your child and not force them to do anything they do not want to do.

Just like a funeral, your child's pet memorial service will reflect their unique relationship with the animal and will include those things that are meaningful to them.

Pet remembrances are lifelong celebrations. Every year, your child can celebrate their pet's birthday by lighting a candle and having a small ceremony. They can also go to their pet's gravesite and leave a favorite toy. This will all depend on the age and development of your child. Often pet remembrances are more important for the adult than the child. Yet, having your child watch you continue to pay tribute will only help them feel comfortable with death and honoring feelings as they become adults.

I encourage the parents that work with me to celebrate in some way throughout the child's life if appropriate by remembering their pet on a special day. It doesn't have to be a big deal. It could be as simple as asking your child, "Today was Jackson's birthday, do you remember how Jackson loved his birthday cookie? What made you laugh when we gave him that cookie?"

Important Points for Planning

Here are some points you may wish to consider as you help your child plan their own unique ceremony of remembrance for their pet, always taking into account your child's age and maturity-level (chapter 3 and 4).

- Take some time to plan what you'd like to do. Involve all family members, including your child and others who may be willing to help you.

- Ask your child whether they want to hold a funeral, a memorial service, or both.

- Given your family's religious beliefs, traditions, and rituals, determine whether you want to include any religious aspects or whether you consider their inclusion inappropriate.

- Think of ways the service can be personalized for your child. At the service ask family members and friends who knew your child's pet to reminisce or recall what was special about the pet.

- Decide who will hold the service, where, when it will be held, who will speak, and who will be invited to attend.

- Know that it is both normal and healthy to use a funeral or memorial service to help your child express their sorrow, proclaim their love, and bid a final farewell to their cherished friend.

Chapter Wrap-Up

In this chapter we covered why it is important for your child to celebrate a pet's life with a pet funeral, memorial, and/or remembrance. You learned the difference between the three and heard the story of Liam, Emma, Charlotte, and Lily, and how much having a pet funeral helped them with their grief journey. Plus, I supplied you with some important points for planning end-of-life ceremonies.

In the next chapter, you are going to learn some extremely effective ways for your child to heal, celebrate, and honor their pet's life.

Tidbits of Wisdom

1. *Your child will benefit by honoring their pet with a funeral or another kind of end-of-life celebration. Lingering questions will be answered and dialogue will be ongoing from the heart.*

2. *Funerals are ways to celebrate the positive rather than express remorse—we forget that.*

3. *A pet funeral is a portal for your child to understand that death is final in physical nature.*

13. Creative Ways to Celebrate

One of the most important exercises that I share with parents who have children that are experiencing a terminally ill pet or the heartache after their pet has died is to support them with a creative project. Writing a love letter, creating a scrapbook, or crafting a one-page tribute will offer you and your child a healthy way to mourn and celebrate at the same time.

A creative outlet and tribute provides a very special way of healing grief. It is a different way for your child to process death. Telling their companion how much they loved and enjoyed them through a creative outlet and tribute provides a healthy way for them to express their memories, experiences, and gratitude for the things that they shared with their cat, dog, horse, bird, hamster, or rabbit.

In this chapter, you are going to learn about three different ways that your child can celebrate the life of their pet through a very healthy and positive approach. Of course, there are many other ways to create a tribute for a beloved animal companion. The three that I am sharing are the ones most often cited by my clients as engaging and versatile for their children.

Creating a Scrapbook

Looking at pictures with your child of their pet can be a great way to begin creating a safe and inviting space for your child to feel comfortable talking about their companion. It is a non-threatening approach to open the dialogue that has room for sharing stories, laughing, crying, and paying tribute.

A scrapbook is a perfect way for a child who doesn't like to write or draw, yet they can still create something that celebrates and honors their pet. A scrapbook, like all three of these activities, offers a means of transforming the negative feelings into something positive.

Roman and Elaina asked their son, Nico (age nine), to help them put together a scrapbook four weeks after his dog, Dante, died. Roman and Elaina said this activity helped Nico preserve the happy moments and all the activities that he and Dante had shared together. It included photographs, pictures that Nico drew when he was little, and cards that people sent to Nico after Dante died.

Originally when Roman and Elaina had called me, they were concerned about their son because it seemed that no matter how honest or supportive they were with Nico, there was something missing. With my guidance this family created a beautiful tribute to celebrate the love, loyalty, and companionship Dante had provided. Nico was able to feel happiness and saw what he'd experienced with Dante as something positive instead of negative. Creating the scrapbook was a powerful and restorative activity for Nico and his family.

Designing a One-Page Tribute

This is another activity that is beneficial for mourning and celebrating the life your child had with their pet. Like scrapbooks, it is appropriate for any age and can be as elaborate as a child wants. I have had clients create a tribute by painting, drawing, or writing a message in a Word document on the computer. Designing a tribute opens the dialogue between you and your child to continue the motion towards healing their grief.

I had a family that had so much fun with this activity. First, they made popcorn (because their dog, Henry, had loved popcorn), and then everyone sat around the dining room table with their computers. The project was for everyone to create their own one-page tribute to Henry. When the final copies were emailed to me, I could see the joy and love this family had for Henry.

To get them started, I helped the family with guidelines as to what to include in their tribute. Once they began the conversation with one another and reminisced about what Henry meant to each of them, they began to add things that I hadn't suggested. It was a healing experience for them.

Henry provided this family with an incredible bonding experience. Five years later, I heard from the parents, who told me, "Every year on the anniversary of Henry's death we get together and read our tributes at the pet cemetery where Henry is buried. Henry gave us a bonding experience that we needed at the time, and we are forever grateful to him."

Here is what to include for your child to begin making their one-page tribute:

- Paper or Word document on a computer

- A picture of their companion

- A short three-to four-sentence tribute

- A list of nicknames

- Birth date and date of death

- Full name of pet

After all this information is gathered, your child can then begin to design a special one-page tribute that can later be framed. One aspect of this exercise that I find beneficial is tributes are relatively easy to create, fun, and each one is unique.

Writing a Love Letter

Writing a love letter can be done at any age, and it will act as an accumulation of your child's love and thanks from them to their beloved animal companion. It is a proclamation of appreciation, healing, apology (if your child feels the need), and inclusion of anything else that they may want to express. It is your child's way to say goodbye in a meaningful way.

You may be asking, "How is that going to help my child?" This is a common question from parents, and oftentimes writing is not one of children's favorite activities—if your child doesn't like to write, honor that, and try one of the other activities in this chapter instead. Or, as some of my clients do, ask your child what they would like to say, and you write it down for them.

To begin supporting your child with writing a love letter, here are some questions to help them frame the love letter:

Do you remember when we first brought your animal companion home? What happened? How did you feel?

Make a list of everything that you and your pet did together. How old were you and your pet? What exactly were you doing together?

What was the biggest gift that your pet gave you?

What are the things that you loved about your pet?

Here are some letters my clients' children wrote:

Isabelle's (age eight) letter that she wrote to Freddie, her hamster—

Dear Freddie,

I really liked to watch you when I was doing my homework, you made me laugh. Homework is boring sometimes, but it wasn't when you made me laugh.

Also I thought you were really pretty. I liked your spots of brown and black, and your whiskers tickled me when I kissed you.

I really miss you, but when I get my next hamster, I am going to tell them all about you.

I love you, Freddie—you were my best friend.

Love and Kisses,

Isabelle

Erin's (age eleven) letter to Crystal, her cat—

Dear Crystal,

You are the best Crystal, and there will never be a cat as great as you. Your white fur was so beautiful, and I didn't mind taking care of you at all.

Some of my friends thought it was gross to clean out your litter box, but I know you were very clean. It was important for you to have your litter box clean. I hope you enjoyed that I did that for you like I think you did.

I also liked the game we played together every day when I got home from school. You would be hiding and I would have to find you. When I did, I loved to hear you purring.

I miss you every day and I will never forget you. Thank you.

Love your people sister,

Erin

Chapter Wrap-Up

In this chapter we talked about creative ways that your child can celebrate the love they had for their animal companion. There are many imaginative and encouraging projects that allow children to express themselves and pay tribute to their pets. The three that I listed in this chapter are favorite choices of my clients' children.

When you find a creative project that suits your child's personality, trust that it will facilitate an open dialogue for them to express their grief in a very healthy manner. The tribute that they create for their animal friend will be a lasting memorial to celebrate the relationship they had with their pet.

When our children celebrate the lives of their pets, they are learning respect for other living beings that they share life with. This invaluable lesson can have a tremendous effect on future choices as children grow into adulthood.

In the next chapter we are going to explore the considerations behind reaching a decision in regard to the very common and significant question, "When should we get another pet for our child and family?" I'll share eight important considerations to keep in mind when making this decision—as well as some case studies that demonstrate how various families decided what was best for them and their child.

Tidbits of Wisdom

1. *By encouraging creativity in your child you are supporting the celebration of life they had with their animal companion.*

2. *A pet memorial tribute will create a lifelong memory for your child.*

3. *Honoring a child's pet provides a special way for them to heal their grief.*

14. Getting Another Pet

"When should we get another pet for our child and family?" is an important and very common question that my clients ask. As I always tell my clients—there is no hard and fast rule about this decision as it has many factors to consider.

Not only will you be thinking of the wellbeing of your child, but consider too where you and your family are in your own stages of grief. The last thing you would want to do is to bring another animal into your home and find that you still have not processed your own grief.

Since there is a lot to consider—the age of your child, what type of pet the child had and now wants, and when you are ready for a new family member, keep in mind that it is okay to take a break. This is one of those perfect teaching moments that a pet provides—the time to talk and reflect with your child about what their pet taught them.

First and foremost, when you are ready to bring another pet into the household, consider the needs and feelings of your child. As you probably already have experienced, your child built a very strong attachment to their pet that died, and they may feel that if they give their love to a new pet, it might be disloyal to the pet that died.

You can decide instead to take your time about getting another pet. Consider this break as another perfect time for you to explain how their previous pet taught them about nurturing, comfort, care, etc., which we discussed in chapter 1.

Next, make sure all family members, including you, have had a chance to work through the individual grieving process (chapter 7). When everyone is ready, you can start a family discussion about what sort of pet to get. If possible, allow your child a special voice in selecting the new pet.

This consideration period can allow them to learn to research the pet they most want. They may want an entirely different type of pet, so by allowing them to research the care and needs of a certain pet, they partake in a valuable learning experience.

However, since the loss of our pets is inescapable because their lifespans are not as long as ours, introducing a new pet to the family doesn't lessen the pain of loss for your child or your family. The grief is still going to be felt.

For some of my clients, opening their hearts to a new dog, cat, or other type of animal, and bringing them into the home soon after a beloved animal companion dies, is extremely helpful. Yet, for other clients, it can take a long time before their child is ready. It is paramount that you recognize at this point if the decision is based on your feeling of grief or your child's readiness.

Remember in chapters 6 and 7 when I talked about how grief has a life of its own, how it is unique to your child, and how everyone is different with how they process grief? Making a decision to get another pet is a personal choice for you and your child to make.

Take your time and listen to what your heart is telling you. Look at the practical considerations, such as finances and the appropriate type of pet to bring into your home, and revisit where you are in your stage of grief to determine if you, as the parent, are ready.

My clients Aaron and Quinn couldn't imagine a home without a family pet, and they remedied it very quickly after their son Blake's cat, Cool, died. Blake (age 12) had a hard time when he came home from school and didn't have the comforting feel of Cool, weaving in and out of his legs and purring all the while. To Aaron, Quinn, and Blake, getting a new cat quickly eased Blake's sadness and brought joy and purpose to him. For them it was the right choice.

Yet, my clients Robert and Sara and their son, James (age 12), needed time to grieve the loss of their cat, Ivy, much longer before James felt he was ready to adopt another cat. James just didn't want to rush into getting another cat because he thought it would not be fair to Ivy.

Though some children, like Blake, want a new cat right away, and others, like James, prefer to wait for a long time, there are other children that have no timeframe. They make the choice to wait until the right pet comes along.

Things to Keep in Mind

1. When welcoming another pet into your family, no matter where your child is with their grief, this action can trigger feelings of loss that you thought your child may have already dealt with. It can challenge your child to deal with

some grief feelings on a deeper level, which can be uncomfortable, surprising, and uninvited.

2. There is no right or wrong time to bring another pet into your family. It's really up to your child and your family as a whole. There are some things to consider to be sure that your child is truly ready, but there are no hard and fast rules to making this decision.

3. Try not to make a hasty decision. Give your child and yourself time to grieve and think. Don't let anyone tell you what the right decision is or pressure you into getting a pet.

4. Your new pet should not be considered a "replacement" for the previous pet. Replacement relationships are not healthy. When your child builds a new relationship with a new pet, those teaching experiences, memories, and experiences will be different, unique, and very special.

5. It is important to involve all family members in the decision to invite a new pet into the household. In particular, consider the needs and feelings of your children. They can easily feel that having a new pet in the home can be disloyal to the previous pet. Everyone in the family needs to have their chance to properly grieve.

6. Since your child's new pet begins a new relationship with everyone in the family, it can be very difficult with healing grief by naming the new pet the same name as the previous pet's. Try and come up with a new name that reflects the personality of that pet and their special antics, personality, or physical features, etc.

7. Having the expectation that the new pet will learn, do, respond, or have the same characteristics as the previous pet is not respectful to your child's new pet. As an alternative encourage your child to experience their new pet as a unique character with a ton of love, fun, and enjoyment. Allow them to feel excited by the differences and quirkiness.

8. If you have other pets in the house, consider if they might enjoy or resent a new pet. Some pets will mourn the loss of a companion, and it will be important for their health and wellbeing to teach your child ways to support the grief of the surviving pet.

Just like the case studies in this chapter and the "Things to Keep in Mind" that I listed above, whether or not to introduce a new pet into your home really depends on how comfortable you and your child are with the stage of grief that you both are in (chapter 7). If you feel that grief no longer affects the way you both experience your daily lives, you can easily bring another pet into your child's life and your home.

When my clients tell me they were at the humane society and found the perfect pet yet question if the time is right, I remind them to step back, take a breath, and trust what they are feeling in their hearts and what they discussed with their child. If there is confusion or doubt, it may mean they are still not ready—and that is okay. Yet, if the "heart-melt" overcomes the uncertainty, this may be the perfect time for you and your child to bring a new pet home.

Finally, if you are not convinced whether your child and you are ready for a new pet, there is always the option to volunteer or at least make some visits to your local humane society. You would be able to spend time cuddling, socializing, and maybe even fostering a pet in need. Your child will be able to share the love in their heart and receive comfort and nurturing they might still need due to the death of their pet. This is an excellent way for them to experience the power of animals and possibly discover a new companion.

Chapter Wrap-Up

In this chapter you learned how to explore and feel confident when choosing to bring home a new pet for your child. You understand the importance of knowing where your child and family are in the stages of grief and how this can affect the decision. Plus you received eight "Things to Keep in Mind" when contemplating this decision.

You heard the stories of Aaron, Quinn, and Blake, and how it was important for them to get a new cat right away after Cool died. Yet, Robert, Sara, and James decided to wait until they processed their grief and gave it time without getting another cat so soon after Ivy died. Both of these families made decisions, though differing, about getting new pets when the time was right for them.

Next in "Final Tidbits of Wisdom" we will talk about the magical bond and innate healing ability that pets have with children. When children experience growing up with a companion animal, they experience a profound connection. Pets create balance and grounding for children and the opportunity for them to grow into remarkable adults.

Tidbits of Wisdom

1. *Taking your time to invite another pet into your child's life is okay. Wait for the heart-melt to happen between your child and the new pet.*

2. *Even though the new pet will provide joy and happiness for your child, stay aware of the unexpected grief that may resurface.*

3. *There is always room in the heart to have another pet. Don't let the pain of grief stop you . . . your child will appreciate your moving on from your own grief, which will allow them to flourish too.*

Final Tidbits of Wisdom

Adding a furry, finned, or feathered friend to your child's life can be a wonderful teaching experience for them and your family. A pet can teach your child simple, yet important life lessons, and the profound experience called the cycle of life.

We can't deny that children and animals share a remarkable bond that is strong and unbreakable. In fact, it is downright magical at times. Have you experienced your child talking to an ant or to their hamster? Sharing with their dog those deep secrets, details of their adventures, and celebrating their joy of learning something new?

These are the special occasions that your child will remember and cherish as they grow into adulthood when they grow up with a companion animal. Having a pet in your child's life can encourage and support them with healthy adventures, life lessons, responsibilities, comfort and safety, the learning of new skills, and the building of family bonds.

Together, a companion animal and your child can give each other an incredible sense of belonging, purpose, and joy. Your child's pet will introduce your child to other people, nature, the universe, and new ways of looking at life. Their pet can give them stability when they couldn't get this need met from family, friends, and teachers. Children and their pets can make each other's life full of purpose, a little easier, and much more fun.

Yet, there will also be a time when your child's pet will offer a most profound experience—teaching your child that all living things must die. Since children are naturally curious and want to know how things work, they will experience various emotions and stages of grief and loss that can be extremely difficult for them to comprehend—having a pet will help them in these areas too. Pets are compassionate, honest teachers for pet loss and provide opportunities for healing. Having you, as their parent, to support their journey is paramount.

Since animals have this innate healing power, their ability to comfort through unconditional love will ease the hard-knocks of life and will give your child strength and courage to move through life with direction. It doesn't matter what type of pet you choose for your child, if they have a strong bond with that pet, their partnership will grow into an amazing learning experience for everyone involved.

The idea that all life ends is a concept that your child may have yet to experience. It is probably the most difficult truth we have to share with our children. Since children flourish with honesty and creativity, there are ways that you can help them talk about and engage with what they are feeling. Their pets will help you.

An honest answer may seem harsh or even cruel, and it may seem easier to answer a child's questions by hiding the truth. Of course, you don't want your child to hurt and you want to protect them. Yet, when you are honest about death, your words will only build love and trust in your child. Plus, you will help them develop into healthy and well-adjusted adults.

Teach your children well, by including a companion animal in their life. Your child will receive advance training with important components for a healthy adulthood—nurturing and developing seeds of love, compassion, and honesty. These are the nutrients they need to develop deep respect for, and kinship with, their environment and the world around them.

Since we tend to avoid talking about things that upset us—dying being one of these topics—we as adults tend to bottle it up and hope if we don't say anything, it will go away. Since your child and, in fact, all children are sensitive indicators of emotions and behaviors, their ability to be keen observers surpasses ours. They know when something is wrong just by watching us. Our body language, facial expressions, what we say and don't—are all things that we are communicating to our children.

To help diminish your child's observing any confusing or negative emotions in your family, I urge you to openly discuss death with your child as their pet is reaching the end of life. Model healthy behaviors as expressed in this book and show them that it is okay to acknowledge and feel sad about the loss of their companion animal.

You can expect that you and your child are going to feel chaotic, isolated, irritated, ravenous, perplexed, bewildered, mixed-up, and all the other normal and common feelings of grief. That is okay and to be expected. Just breathe and listen as you support them with healing their pet loss grief.

In order to soothe their soul, keep in mind that their bond with their pet was not shared by anyone else. It was entirely exclusive and exceptional to your child. Therefore, what they experience after the death of their companion animal is going to reflect their personality, their pet's personality, and all the things they shared together.

Be ready for the fact that you will be faced with some tough and challenging decisions that will demand your attention to tell the truth. You want to be able to make these decisions without regret, guilt, or remorse.

Your job now is to help your child mourn and experience the changes in their life. Help them learn from the experience they had and ultimately help them fill their heart again.

Allow and support your child to mourn their emotions and celebrate the life they had with their companion with supportive and non-judgmental activities, friends, family, support groups, or a pet loss coach.

The changes that your child is now experiencing and their feelings of grief can result in a tremendous impact in the way they move through life. This book took you by the hand and supported you with tools and options on how you can help your child from choosing the perfect pet to experiencing in a healthy way the end of that pet's life—teaching and guiding you with valuable and golden lessons the entire way.

Please visit my website, which is listed in the "Resources" section of this book. There are many services that you will see listed that will help you and your child with the next step after reading this book. You can continue to receive support from me as you continue the journey.

Amy (age twelve), whose dog Peach died, said to me after she and her mom finished my program, *Rescue Joy From Pet Loss Grief*:

> *Wendy, I was really sad when Peach died. I didn't want to go to school or play with my friends. Peach was my best friend, and she slept in my bed at night. I was really lonely. When Mom and I found you on the Internet, I was nervous at first, but you were so nice. You listened to me, helped me, and gave me some fun things to do. I drew really nice pictures of Peach that are on my wall in my bedroom. If I feel sad, I just look at those pictures and I feel better. Thank you. You would have loved Peach too.*

Like Amy, your child can have a safe and calm place to talk about what they are experiencing. By providing them with inspiration, respect, honesty, and understanding, your child will learn to have a different connection with their companion animal that will last a lifetime.

Final Tidbit of Wisdom

All children will benefit by sharing their lives with a companion animal. They will greatly flourish by developing and maintaining a heart-felt compassion that is as reflexive as breathing. A pet will share these lessons with your child forever—through life, death, and beyond.

Resources

Ways That I Can Support You

Center for Pet Loss Grief: Through Life, Death, and Beyond
Wendy Van de Poll, MS, CEOL

> *A free gift from my heart to yours awaits you!*
> https://www.centerforpetlossgrief.com/

Free Pet Grief Support Kit
https://centerforpetlossgrief.com

Animal Mediumship
https://centerforpetlossgrief.com/animal-medium

Animal Communication
https://wendyvandepoll.com/animal-communication

Pet Funerals
https://centerforpetlossgrief.com/pet-funeral

Facebook
Center for Pet Loss Grief
https://facebook.com/centerforpetlossgrief

Pet Memorial Support Group
https://facebook.com/groups/petmemorials.
centerforpetlossgrief

Blog Articles Mentioned in This Book

Article about the 7 stages of grief that adults may experience
https://www.centerforpetlossgrief.com/grief-and-loss-stages-for-pet-loss/

Article about common myths concerning grief that adults may experience
https://www.centerforpetlossgrief.com/myths-of-healing-pet-loss-myth-one-2/

Article about adult experience of mourning for a pet
https://www.centerforpetlossgrief.com/mourning-a-pet/

Books

Ages 0–2
Goodbye Mousie by Robi H. Harris
Goodbye by Todd Parr

Ages 4–8
Murphy and Kate by Ellen Howard
Lifetimes: The Beautiful Way to Explain Death to Children
    by Bryan Mellonie
Chester Raccoon and The Acorn Full of Memories
    by Audrey Penn
The Tenth Good Thing About Barney by Judith Viorst

Ages 8–12
Umbrella Summer by Lisa Graff
Binny for Short by Hilary McKay
End of Life Rituals by World Book, Inc
The Leanin' Dog by K.A. Nuzum

Veterinarians:

Veterinary Medical Association
www.ahvma.org/

Home Euthanasia and Pet Hospice Veterinarians
www.iaahpc.org/

Online Product Support:

Herbal Support: Pet Wellness Blends Affiliate
www.herbs-for-life-3.myshopify.com/#_l_1e

Magnetic Therapy Supplies: aVivoPur Affiliate
www.avivopur.com/#_a_CenterForPetLossGrief

Heart in Diamonds: Affiliate
www.heart-in-diamonds.com/?aff=CenterForPetLoss

Support Groups:

Association for Pet Loss and Bereavement
www.aplb.org/

International Association for Animal Hospice and Palliative Care
www.iaahpc.org/

Association for Human-Animal Bond Veterinarians
www.aahabv.org/

Acknowledgments

First, I would love to express my deepest compassion to all the children who shared with me their stories of when their pets died. I heard amazing things from these children—some so profound they taught me new lessons about how death gives way for life.

I would also like to thank their parents who felt confident to trust me to walk the challenging journey of healing pet loss with them and their children. Together, we covered a lot of ground.

I would also like to shout out to the folks at Self Publishing School that have guided me to follow my lifelong passion of becoming a bestselling author. My SPS family, RE Vance, and my launch team members are the best!

I am truly in awe of my editor, Nancy Pile, who once again added her heart and paws to bring my book to another level. To Debbie Lum for her beautiful formatting, and to Danijela Mijailovic for her gorgeous book cover artistry.

To Addie, Marley, Kado, Maya, and the rest of my fur, feather, and fin gurus who continue to hold my heart through vital life lessons and goals that I am determined to accomplish. They are amazing and wise teachers. They never let me forget who I am.

And, of course, to my crazy and wonderful hubby! Your dedication to me is appreciated and loved with every cell of my body.

About the Author

Wendy Van de Poll is a pioneering leader in the field of pet loss grief support. Wendy is dedicated to providing a safe place for her clients to express their grief over the loss of their pets.

What makes Wendy successful with her clients is that she get's grief! *"Over the years I've dealt with my own grief and helping many families communicate and connect with their pets long after their loss. It's what I've done since I was just 5 yrs old!"*

She is compassionate and supportive to all who know her.

Her passion is to help people when they are grieving over the loss of a pet and her larger than life love for animals has led her to devote her life to the mission of increasing the quality of life between animals and people no matter what stage they are in their cycle of life! She has been called the animal whisperer.

She is a Certified End of Life and Pet Grief Support Coach, Certified Pet Funeral Celebrant, Animal Medium and Communicator. She is the founder of The Center for Pet Loss Grief and an international best selling and award-winning author and speaker.

She holds a Master's of Science degree in Wolf Ecology and Behavior and has run with wild wolves in Minnesota, coyotes in Massachusetts and foxes in her backyard. She lives in the woods with her husband, two crazy birds, her rescue dog Addie and all kinds of wildlife.

Wendy currently has a Skype, phone, and in person practice, providing end-of-life and pet grief support coaching, gentle massage and energy healing for animals, animal mediumship, and personalized pet funerals.

You can reach her at www.centerforpetlossgrief.com.

Thank You for Reading

Healing a Child's Pet Loss Grief
A Guide for Parents

Marley with some of her friends

This was a very special book for me to write. I had the opportunity to talk with parents and children all over the world about the magic of their pets, sharing hearts as I supported these children with their grief and honoring the life they created with their animal companions.

It would mean a lot if you left a review on Amazon because it would show other parents searching for help—parents like you—there is a book to guide them with healing their child's pet loss grief journey.

My goal for this book is to help as many parents and children as I can with love, compassion, and honesty. I want to show parents how to heal their child's heart, allowing it to mend through the power of animals.

I would be grateful if you would leave a helpful REVIEW on Amazon using this link: http://a.co/cvWsCDK.

Thank you,

Wendy

The Pet Bereavement Series
Best Selling and Award Winning Books

By Wendy Van de Poll, MS, CEOL

My Dog IS Dying: What Do I Do?
My Dog HAS Died: What Do I Do?

My Cat IS Dying: What Do I Do?
My Cat HAS Died: What Do I Do?

Healing A Child's Pet Loss Grief

Free Book

Healing Your Heart From Pet Loss Grief

To receive notification when more books are published, please go to https://www.centerforpetlossgrief.com/, and we'll include you on the mailing list after you download your free gift.

Made in the USA
Columbia, SC
05 May 2019